SAN DIEGO PUBLIC LIBRARY

3 1336 01911 5550

ID0960574

STORAGE   5550

081 Grizzard, L
        Won't you come home,
     Billy Bob Bailey?
                           995

FEB 5 1986

SAN DIEGO PUBLIC LIBRARY

**ALWAYS BRING YOUR
CARD WITH YOU.**

Published by
PEACHTREE PUBLISHERS, LTD.
494 Armour Circle, N. E.
Atlanta, Georgia 30324

Copyright © 1980 Lewis Grizzard

All rights reserved. No part of this book may be reproduced in any form
or by any means without the prior written permission of the Publisher,
excepting brief quotes used in connection with reviews, written
specifically for inclusion in a magazine or newspaper.

Manufactured in the United States of America

Text and Cover Design by Joan Stoliar

Library of Congress Cataloging in Publication Data

Grizzard, Lewis, 1946—
   Won't you come home, Billy Bob Bailey?

   I. Title.
AC8.G949   081   80-23407
ISBN 0-931948-10-X
8th printing

To Kathy,
Who loves me anyway

contents

1

Take My Advice . . . Please!

2

Famous People You Have Never Heard Of

3

Great Issues

1

Take My Advice...
Please!

Grits
Billy
Bob

There are probably some things more important than learning how to cook good grits—or, learning how to cook grits good—but I can't think of any off the top of my head, so that is why this book begins with the following piece, written by my good friend, Billy Bob Bailey of Fort Deposit, Alabama.

Billy Bob writes my newspaper column for me occasionally, like when I have to get a haircut, and he has become quite popular with my readers, except those who are from the North. They are quite offended by Billy Bob.

Of course, they don't like grits, either, which is how all the following got started in the first place.

my name is Billy Bob Bailey, and I live down in Fort Deposit, Alabama, which ain't close to nothing but the ground. Plumbing maintenance is my game—you name it and I can unstop it—but on the side I write a newspaper column for the local weekly.

It's called "The Straight Flush with Billy Bob." My dog Rooster's the one who thought up that name.

Me and Lewis Grizzard go way back. We knew each other

3

before Studebaker went broke. He's a good ol' boy, Lewis, but he's bad to get into what I call one of his sorry spells. Too sorry to work, and too sorry to care if he don't.

If his hind end ever gets any weight on it, they ought to hang the lazy scoundrel.

So here I am bailin' him out again while he takes another day off. I bet his time card's got more empty spaces on it than the doctors saw when they examined the Penn State football team for brain damage after it was run slap over by the University of Aladamnbama in the Sugar Bowl.

We're still celebrating knocking Four-Eyed Joe Paterno out of the national championship. It's true we got us an Auburn man sittin' in the governor's chair in Montgomery now, but it's Mr. Paul Bryant who's still the king, roll Tide.

Football ain't what's on my mind today, though, but I've got something to talk about that's just about as important.

Grits.

You heard me right. G—for "good"—r-i-t-s, grits. This all started a week ago when me and Rooster went down to the diner to have breakfast.

Sittin' in the diner were these two Yankee tourists who got lost trying to find Florida, which ain't exactly hard to locate like Rhode Island or Kansas. You just drive that big black Buick until everybody you see is two years older than Lydia E. Pinkham's hat.

Clovis, the waitress, asked the two Yankees if they wanted grits with their eggs, and they turned up their noses and said they'd rather eat mud first.

Clovis blanched, and it was all I could do to keep Rooster still. I don't know why it is people from up North who come South want to make fun of the way we eat and talk.

Before I got down in my back, I used to have a special way of dealing with riff-raff like that. After they got out of the hospital,

4

they couldn't wait to get back to New Jersey where it smells like what it took me half a day to unclog at the bus station last week.

But Billy Bob ain't as young as he used to be, and I'm learning to be a little more tolerant about ignorance. This is a free country, and if somebody ain't got the good sense God gave a sweet potato, it ain't up to me to move his nose over to the side a little.

The reason Yankees don't like grits is nobody ever told 'em how to eat 'em. If you don't doctor up grits a little, I'll be the first to admit they taste like something I wouldn't even say.

Grits need a little help, and what I'm going to do today is give out my famous recipe for Grits Billy Bob, and if you have anything to do with any Yankees, you might pass it along.

Grits Billy Bob:

First, don't fool with no instant grits. The idiot who invented instant grits also thought of frozen fried chicken, and they ought to lock him up before he tries to freeze-dry collards.

Get yourself some Aunt Jemimas or some Jim Dandys. Cook 'em slow and stir every chance you get. Otherwise, you'll have lumps, and you don't want lumps.

Salt and pepper and stir in enough butter to choke a goat. Fry some bacon and sausage on the side and crumble that in, and then come right on top of that with all the cheese the law will allow.

Grits Billy Bob ought not to *run* out of the pot. They ought to *crawl*. Serve hot. Cold Grits Billy Bob are harder than a steel-belted radial.

Speaking of tires, it was a shame the bad luck those two Yankees had before they could get out of town. All four of their tires blew out right in front of Clovis's brother's service station. His name is Harvey.

Harvey made 'em a good deal on a new set, though. Said he never had seen tires punctured that way. Said they looked like something with real sharp teeth had gnawed right through 'em.

Rooster said he figured they ran over a possum.

5

On
Living
Alone

This was written before I got marrried—again—
which will all be explained at the end of the book.
But for those of you who are still living alone, or
who are planning to give it a try, there should be
some excellent advice for you here. Like the part
about underwear. Clean underwear doesn't grow on
trees, you know.

i'm not certain who digs up such information, or who pays
for the digging, but there was an item on the evening news about
more and more Americans living alone these days.

I can think of at least three reasons for that:

1. People are waiting around longer before they get
married.

2. Those who didn't wait around to get married are getting
divorced in droves.

3. Maybe there are more nurdy-type people who can't find
anybody who will live with them.

I am sort of an expert on all this because I live alone. I could
go into details as to why, but that isn't really necessary. Just check
somewhere between aforementioned reasons-for-living-alone
"2" and "3."

A lot of people actually enjoy living alone. There are certain
advantages:

1. People who live alone can leave their underwear lying
around all over the floor.

2. There are never any arguments over what to watch on television. If you live alone, you can even watch "The Dating Game," and who will know?

3. The phone is always for you.

4. You never have to hear, "Honey, there's something I've been meaning to talk to you about," when Dallas is fourth-and-one on the Washington two-yard line.

5. If you find a hair in your soup, you know for certain whose it is.

I could go on, but those are the highlights. Perhaps what I am trying to say is, if you are sharing a dwelling and think you would like to kick the bum or old bag out, think twice.

The item on the evening news went on to say people who live alone tend to die younger than others.

I think I know why. I can only speak for the male of the species, but there are certain shocks that will come the minute she's gone, fellows.

Let's go back to the underwear for a second. You probably think your underwear walks to the washing machine, dives in, and after washing itself, marches back to your dresser, gets inside, and folds itself.

Soon after I was cast adrift, I wore all my underwear once, and then looked in the dresser for another fresh pair. My underwear was where I had left it—lying around all over the floor.

A man of my standing and upbringing certainly wasn't going to wash his own underwear, so I did a second-time-around on the dirties. After that I had no choice. I went to K-Mart where they were having a special and bought a six-month supply of under-shorts.

When they were dirty, I did what any other just-divorced American male would do. I threw them away and bought another six-month supply.

7

There are other similar problems. Toilet paper and fresh towels don't grow in the bathroom. Strange green things do if you don't clean it, however.

Light bulbs. Light bulbs will drive you crazy. They are always burning out. You have to take the time from your busy schedule to go out and BUY more light bulbs and then bring them home and screw them in. That alone can take years off your life.

Food. You live alone, you try cooking for yourself. You cook for yourself, you can get poisoned, and then there are the dishes. You don't cook, you eat a lot of heat-and-serve Mexican dinners, which annually kill thousands of men who live alone.

Beer cans. Who is going to throw his own beer cans in the garbage? Let me tell you something about beer cans. You leave a couple of empty beer cans around, and the next time you look there will be four beer cans, and then eight, and, pretty soon, you are up to your eyeballs in empty beer cans.

If you are about to strike out alone, big boy, I don't mean to frighten you with this, so to soften the blow, maybe I should offer one more advantage to living by yourself:

If you do happen to die young, maybe the end will come before you finally have to break down and change your sheets.

8

The Truth About Dentists

Nearly every society has had its element of cruel and sadistic monsters, preying on the helpless and innocent. We call ours "dentists."

get ready for this, because I don't want you to be caught off guard. The American Dental Association has launched a new propaganda scheme aimed at people who will do anything to stay out of a dentist's office—people like me.

We are no small group. According to its own figures, the ADA says only half the population goes to the dentist each year.

The purpose of its scheme is to get the other 50 percent strapped into that chair so the dentist can scrape and pull and drill and make the poor suckers hurt and bleed and then charge them for his trouble.

The scheme includes sending out ADA "ambassadors" all over the country to tell you incredible lies, such as, it doesn't hurt to go to the dentist anymore.

One of those "ambassadors" is a lady dentist named Dr. Sheva Rapoport, of Allentown, Pennsylvania. I read a newspaper account of some of the baloney she is peddling.

Get a load of this song and dance. According to Dr. Rapoport:

● Dentists' offices now offer a more pleasant environment than before.

● Dentists are now more aware of their patients' feelings.

9

- Dental equipment has been improved.
- If you ask for one, a dentist will provide a cost estimate before he starts excavating in your mouth.

Big deal. So dentists have put in Muzak and hung a few pictures, and now you can find out about their outrageous prices ahead of time.

What the ADA wants to do is to double root-canal sales, and I, for one, will not be fooled by its would-be clever trick.

Do not listen to the ADA, America. Listen to your Uncle Lewis, who knows all there is to know about dentists, because he was held prisoner by one until he was old enough to escape without parental consent.

The *truth* about dentists—clip and save:

- Of course, it still hurts to go to the dentist, because dentists WANT it to hurt. They like to watch you squirm, they like to hear your muffled cries of agony, they like to fill your mouth with cotton and then ask you, So who do you like Monday night? The Cowboys or the Steelers?
- Dental equipment will be improved only when the heinous drill is totally silent, has a rubber tip, and tickles, rather than feels like someone has taken to your mouth with the first cousin to a jackhammer.
- When a dentist says, "This may sting a little," he really means, "How high can you jump?"
- Oral Roberts University is not a school of dentistry.
- Beware any dentist whose nickname is "Mad Dog" or "Nick the Grinder."
- Beware any dentist with a nervous twitch.
- Beware any dentist who is missing one or more fingers.
- Beware any dentist who is wearing an inordinate amount of leather and whose chair has straps.
- Beware dating dental assistants. They kiss with their teeth, and floss in public.

10

● Despite what the American Dental Association says, there are worse things than having all your teeth rot out.

● I would gladly list a couple, but it's late and I have to go gum dinner.

Learning to
Mix With
the Idle Rich

*I am the only person in my family ever to have spent
a weekend at The Cloister on Sea Island, or
anywhere like it. However, my Uncle Gaylord once
spent a weekend in Tulsa, where he finished second
in a pool tournament and met his fourth wife, who
was performing on the tables in the motel lounge.
Uncle Gaylord always knew how to live.*

Sea Island, Ga.

Soon, I will be checking out of The Cloister, a famous resort
hotel for rich people. Soon, I will be penniless again.

A weekend here costs four houses and a mortgage on Marvin
Gardens. Harley Devonshire Billups III, the big butter and egg
man from Shreveport, might have that kind of stash, but I was
hoping somebody would put me on scholarship before settle-up
time came at the cashier's window in the lobby.

This place is so spiffy, you have to wear a tuxedo for tennis. The
Cloister, people always say, is full of "old world charm." That
means that if you don't own at least one small European country,
you'll choke when you see your bill.

The bigs come here. Corporation presidents, heads of state,
politicians who haven't been caught yet, and wealthy baseball
players like Pete Rose, would come, if they had any class.

All weekend, I have felt like a leisure suit at the club's spring
formal. What if the other guests, I kept asking myself, discover a
charlatan has slipped into their midst?

I took extra precautions, like wearing dark socks and parking the truck off the island, but rich people can usually sniff out a taxpayer. We fold our wallets inside out.

One fellow almost caught me over drinks in one of the club rooms. He was from New York and several other places. I think he owned Canada or something.

"What's your game, old chap?" he asked me.

"Newspapers," I said.

"Buying or selling?" he persisted.

I took a long sip from my drink, a Rednecker. That's an amaretto straight-up with a long-neck Bud chaser.

"Buying," I said, which isn't a total lie. When I can't rip off my daily copy from the boss's office, I have to pop for a quarter and go to the rack like everyone else.

There is a lot to do at The Cloister, located on the opulent Golden Isles of Georgia and a million miles from the back room of Harold's Barbecue in Atlanta, one of my other favorite vacation spots.

You can go for a walk on the beach, or play tennis, golf, croquet, lawn bowls, shuffleboard, and bridge. You can shoot skeet at the gun club, go horseback riding, take dancing lessons, or drink afternoon tea with the older folk.

It is true that a lot of older people do visit here. In fact, the line on The Cloister goes, it's the spot for "newlyweds and nearly-deads." Often, young couples honeymoon here who fit both categories after a week of bundling in their ocean-front bungalows.

One of the older people I met here was a delightful man they call "The Colonel." The Colonel is a West Pointer, class of '15. Eisenhower was one of his classmates. He is looking forward to his next reunion.

"Only nineteen of us left now," said the Colonel as he gunned down a final prune juice and left for his dancing lesson.

The reason I did this—took a room at The Cloister for the weekend—is I deserved it. The rigors of work have been piling up, the heap I drive blew a gasket, the moths ate another hole in my sportscoat, and I left my favorite Willie Nelson album on a window ledge the other morning and the sun warped it, which is why Willie sounds like Kate Smith with a bucket over her head.

So I came here to get away from it all. I had patio breakfasts overlooking the gray Atlantic. One morning I even ordered Kadota figs fresh from South Kadota. I dined in graceful elegance, played tennis, rubbed and bent elbows with the landed gentry, and dozed in the sunshine with the Colonel.

It's like they say in those beer commercials, "You only go around once . . . " so grab all the cucumber aspic you can.

Besides, next week I can eat the soap I stole off the maid's cleaning cart.

How to
Survive an
Airplane Crash

*A lot of people aren't really serious about their fear
of flying. I am. I once rode a bus from Atlanta to El
Paso and back to avoid flying. Don't knock it. The
bus station in Shreveport, where you stop for dinner,
has terrific meat loaf, which is impossible to find on
any airline in the country.*

a reader who obviously knows of my problems with air
travel has passed along a clipping of an article about how to
survive if you happen to be in one of those winged monsters and
worst comes to absolute worst.

The article is entitled, appropriately enough, "How to
Survive a Plane Crash," by former flight attendant Sarah
Uzzel-Rindlaub, who has miraculously survived two.

I read the article with great interest. There ARE things that
frighten me more than flying—nuclear war, losing my travelers'
checks in Tehran—but not very many.

One, I don't understand flying. I don't understand how
anything that big goes that high and stays up there that long and is
able to come down softly.

Two, I have this thing about being burned to a crisp or
getting separated from myself, both of which can happen in an
airplane crash.

Sarah Uzzel-Rindlaub survived a crash at Kennedy airport
and, six weeks later, another during a landing in Istanbul.

A normal person would take a bus next time. Not Sarah. She is now emergency procedures instructor for United Airlines.

In a couple of words, she says you will have a better shot at living through a plane crash if you "don't panic."

Somehow, I knew she was going to say that. Every time I tell somebody how much it frightens me to ride in an airplane and how afraid I am it will fall out of the sky and I will die, they say, "Don't panic."

I panic dialing the airlines for reservations.

I panic getting a shoeshine before my flight.

In flight, it is Terror City at 30,000 feet.

I dare not eat anything. In order to eat, I would have to loosen my grip on the seat.

I dare not have a conversation with a fellow passenger. I must remain completely quiet in order to listen for changes in engine tone.

I dare not go to the restroom when I fly, either, because once I did. The plane hit turbulence and a light came on in the restroom that said, "Return to your seat immediately."

When you are in the restroom on an airplane, it is not always possible to return to your seat immediately. What did I do? I panicked, of course, but I will spare you the details.

I gave up flying once for six years. I rode a bus through Alabama, took a cross-country train trip or two, and one night I was driving through a lonely stretch of Arkansas and had a blowout, and my jack was bent.

Along came a semi hauling hogs. I hitched a ride to the next town, seventy-five miles away. The stench was awful. Hogs have poor personal hygiene.

"Sorry about that smell," said the driver.

"No problem, good buddy," I replied, "at least I'm not flying."

But it is next to impossible to live in today's fast-paced world without occasionally having to board an airplane.

My first flight after my absence from the skies was leaving at two o'clock in the afternoon. By ten in the morning, I had already broken out in some hideous rash and had checked and rechecked my will.

I decided to call a friend, an ex-Air Force pilot, for encouragement. Perhaps he could calm me.

"I've flown thousands of hours," he began. "If anything happens to the plane, or there is any sign of trouble, just do the following:

"Bend down as far as you can behind the seat in front of you. Grab each ankle securely. Bend your head between your legs, and . . . . "

"I know," I interrupted him, " 'don't panic.' "

"No," he said, "kiss your bohunkus goodby."

I know the reader who sent me Sarah what's-her-name's article was just trying to help. Next time, don't bother; I'm beyond it.

Fun and
Games at
Home

*It could happen, you know. No gasoline, and there
you are, stuck at home. Make the best of it with my
Treasure Chest of Homespun Fun.*

according to an article in the *Wall Street Journal*,
Americans are staying home these days in droves because of the
gasoline shortage.

(For the record, I have never purchased a copy of the *Wall
Street Journal*, but a junior executive friend of mine buys one
every day to wear to work. He passes his copies to me, along with
an occasional pair of dark over-the-calf-socks.)

The *Journal* article said resort areas can expect to start taking
financial beatings because people are beginning to find all sorts of
ways to entertain themselves in their very own homes.

The article mentioned sitting by your pool, watching cable
television and videotape machines, and riding bicycles.

Since the average price of a house is closing in on six figures,
it does make a great deal of sense to spend a little more time
where you get your mail.

Ours is the only country in the world where we pay $150,000
for a house and then leave it for two weeks every summer to go
sleep in a tent.

The obvious problem here, however, is not all of us can
afford swimming pools, cable television and videotape machines,
and riding bicycles is hard work.

I have no swimming pool, no cable television, no videotape

machine; and the last time I rode a bicycle I was twelve and obviously mentally retarded, or I would have known to take a taxi.

But as an experiment in lifestyle-changing, I stayed home a couple of days and entertained myself. I discovered a person doesn't have to go bowling to have a good time.

Right in the comfort of your own home, no matter how modest it might be, you can have loads of fun and tell the Arab oil peddlers to go eat some sand.

What follows is Grizzard's Treasure Chest of Homespun Fun. Planning a trip to Disney World? Who needs it?

Stay home, America, and:

● PLAY WITH THE KIDS: You remember your kids. Skeeter is eleven. Barney is eight. After you have played with your kids for a while, lock the little boogers in a closet and have a couple of belts.

But remember to let them out in time for tomorrow's roof climb and picnic.

● EAT: Fun for the entire family. Instead of three meals a day, eat twelve. If you take an hour for each meal, and an hour in between, that's an entire day and it's time to eat again.

Soon, the opportunity will arise for other fun home games. Like trying to find Mom's original chin. Hide-and-go-seek in Dad's trousers. And pin the tail on the "Whale," baby sister's new nickname.

● TAKE BATHS: Rub-a-dub-dub, just relaxing in the tub. Invite your neighbors. If things go well, you may never want to leave home again.

● CLEAN OUT YOUR ATTIC OR BASEMENT: Who knows what you might find there? Remember your Uncle Fred, who's been missing since 1958? Dust him off and you've got another entry for the houseplant-swallowing tournament.

● STOMPING ANTS: There are always a lot of ants around the house. How many ants can you stomp?

● COUNTING STOMPED ANTS: Tedious as heck, but a great way to relax after stomping a few hundred thousand ants.

● SETTING THE GARAGE ON FIRE: Wow! See the bright red fire engines! Hear the shrill of their sirens! See the brave firemen battle the blaze! See the friendly insurance man deliver the check!

● MEMORIZE THE PHONE BOOK: "Aaron" to "Zzbowski," hours of good, clean fun. Unless, of course, you live in Yellville, Arkansas, where it will take you approximately nine minutes.

● MONOPOLY: Four can play, but Monopoly may have changed a bit since you played it last. "Free Parking" is now a condominium complex, and when you pass "GO" you have to PAY $200.

Also, you can't take a ride on the Reading anymore. With the gasoline shortage, trains are booked solid.

The Pass-the-Maalox Diet

More advice for singles: If you don't cook, follow this simple diet and you'll be dead in a year, which is better than having to face breakfast at McDonald's indefinitely.

there are all sorts of diets to choose from today. Diets for people who are overweight, diets for people who want to live a long time. Scarsdale diets. Pritikin diets.

There is no diet, however, for the segment of our population that is always being left out—the American Single Person Who Lives Alone and Would Probably Starve to Death Were It Not for Chinese Take-Out Restaurants.

I am one of those persons. I am not married, I live alone, and if I eat one more cardboard box full of fried rice and chicken almondine, I may start quacking like a Peking duck.

I do not cook. I cannot cook. I refuse to cook. Cooking takes a lot of time and causes greasy pots. Weird things that are green grow on greasy pots when they are not washed in several weeks.

But I survive, and I still have my slim, boyish figure. Unfortunately, I also still have sunken eyes, protruding ribs, and a daily bout with acid indigestion that would gag Mother Tums.

A lot of people are making a lot of money writing books about their diets. I do not have time to write a book, because I have to finish this in a hurry so I can meet somebody at Long John Silver's for lunch.

Therefore, I will make it quick and simple:

21

The Grizzard Diet for Single Non-Cookers Who Are in a Hurry.

Eat, drink, and be merry, for tomorrow you may get lockjaw and your troubles will be over:

MONDAY

BREAKFAST—Who can eat breakfast on a Monday? Swallow some toothpaste while you are brushing your teeth.

LUNCH—Send your secretary out for six "gutbombers," those little hamburgers that used to cost a dime and now cost thirty-five cents. Also, order French fries, a bowl of chili, a soft drink, and have your secretary stop on the way back for a bottle of Maalox, family size.

AFTERNOON SNACK—Finish off the bottle of Maalox.

DINNER—Six-pack of beer and Kentucky Fried Chicken three-piece dinner. Don't eat the cole slaw.

TUESDAY

BREAKFAST—Eat the cole slaw.

LUNCH—Go to the office vending area and put ninety-five cents into the machine and close your eyes and push a button. Whatever comes out, swallow it whole. Chewing that garbage increases the inevitable nausea.

DINNER—Four tacos and a pitcher of sangria at El Flasho's.

WEDNESDAY

BREAKFAST—"Jaws" couldn't eat breakfast after a night at El Flasho's.

LUNCH—Rolaids and a Pepsi.

DINNER—Drop in at a married friend's house and beg for table scraps.

THURSDAY

BREAKFAST—Order out for pizza.

LUNCH—Your secretary is out sick. Check Monday's "gutbomber" sack for leftovers.

DINNER—Go to a bar and drink yourself silly. When you get hungry, ask the bartender for olives.

FRIDAY

BREAKFAST—Eggs, sausage, and an English muffin at McDonald's. Eat the Styrofoam plate and leave the food. It tastes better and it's better for you.

LUNCH—Skip lunch, Fridays are murder.

DINNER—Steak, well-done, baked potato, and order the asparagus, but don't eat it. Nobody really likes asparagus.

SATURDAY

BREAKFAST—Sleep through it.

LUNCH—Ditto.

DINNER—Steak, well-done, baked potato, and order the Brussels sprouts, but don't eat them. Take them home and plant them in a hanging basket.

SUNDAY

BREAKFAST—Three Bloody Marys and half a Twinkie cake.

LUNCH—Eat lunch, waste a good buzz. Don't eat lunch.

DINNER—Chicken noodle soup. Call your mom, and ask her about renting your old room.

2

Famous People
You Have
Never Heard Of

Mama Willie

Soon after dying, "Mama Willie" went to the heaven it talked about in her Bible, and she is presently very happy there. For some reason, I am absolutely certain of that.

WMoreland, Ga.
illie Smith Word died last week, and they took her down to the little cemetery on the south end of town and put her next to the only man in her life, Charles Bunyon Word, who will have been gone twenty years come April.

Willie Word lived to be almost eighty-nine. She was the mother of five children. I can't begin to count the grandchildren, great-grandchildren, and even great-great-grandchildren.

The funeral was what Willie Word—we called her "Mama Willie"—would have wanted, two hard-shell Baptist preachers shaking the rafters in the tiny church and duet renditions of her favorite hymns, "Amazing Grace" and "Precious Memories."

"I've known this good woman all of my life," one of the preachers said. "She was solid as a rock."

She was. I knew Willie Word all of my life, too. I think you would have liked her.

She laughed a lot. I will always remember that. And she enjoyed a little dip of snuff before bed, and she knew a number of important things she passed along to those fortunate enough to find a place under her wing.

Important things. Like thunder won't hurt you, but running with a pointed object can. Like if you don't take a nap after lunch, you could get polio; and Jesus said the red words in the Bible.

She could cook. The woman never failed at a pie or a cake, and she must have fried 10,000 chickens in her lifetime. I hope I remembered to thank her for the portion that wound up on my plate.

She was born dirt poor in another century. Think of the changes she saw in her eighty-eight-plus years:

Two world wars, the Great Depression, running water, the automobile, the airplane, radio, television, William McKinley to Jimmy Carter, horses and buggies to moon shots.

This was the same woman who never missed a rasslin' match on television and dared anyone to suggest the punches might be pulled.

She saw some troubles. A son died young. Her man went suddenly. And her last years were filled with pain.

She was taken from her little frame house a couple of years ago and hospitalized, never to come home again. There was no hope. But she lingered on and on, barely conscious of her surroundings.

"How she must have suffered," a daughter was saying at the funeral.

The modern technology that can send a man to the moon and can even stall death may be thanked.

Willie Word lingered with only the support of drugs and devices, and perhaps she did suffer; and she died in somebody else's bed, and I think she deserved better.

Who's to blame? We all are, because those prolonging drugs and devices say we still haven't accepted the fact that when a life ceases to be precious, it is an affront to that life not to allow its natural—and dignified—leave.

Mama Willie

My family—and other families in similar situations—might not have wanted to be reminded of that, but I think Willie Smith Word, my grandmother, would have wanted me to say it anyway.

The Lady at the Diner

I've heard a lot of highly-educated women say that what's wrong with most men is we go around looking for somebody to mother us all the time. They're right, you know. We do.

She sits there behind the cash register every day with her bad leg, and she takes the money from the people who have been through the line and filled their plates with the wonders of Southern cooking.

They ruin us early in the South. Our mothers do it. Heaping plates of country-fried steak, smothered in gravy, and the like. And when they cook vegetables, they cook them in conjunction with something known as "fatback," which is something left over from a pig, and the resulting taste defies description.

And we are taught not to leave a morsel. There was a fellow I knew from Alabama who tried to explain his 400-pound frame.

"I grew up during the war," he said. "Every night, my mother would fill my plate and say, 'Don't leave anything, son. Every time you leave something on your plate, you're wasting food and feeding Hitler.'

"Hell, I tried to starve the entire German army."

We never quite get over that. We leave our mothers' tables and then we roam endlessly in search of a reasonable facsimile of her servings, and more often than not, the search is fruitless.

That is why the lady behind the cash register and her little diner down in a shaky part of town are so important to me.

30

The food is genuine. Monday is spare ribs. Tuesday is the country-fried steak, praise the Lord. Wednesday might be fried chicken, Thursday is ham and maybe some homemade chicken pot pie, and on Friday there's fried fish, and every day the string beans and the squash with onions and the baby limas will take your breath.

The lady behind the register was gone for a time with the leg, and her husband, as gentle and kind as she, handled both their duties. Now she is back, but he is gone with an illness of his own.

And the neighborhood is going down as the crime rate in the city soars.

Derelicts line the sidewalks and pass around their paper sacks with the drunken dreams inside. Gangs of toughs are all about.

I stopped in the diner last week and took a corner booth.

Three urchins from the street, eight or nine or ten, had entered through a side door. Near the line of food is a counter of candies and tobaccos. The smallest of the three snatched something and then bolted for the door.

It was a nickel crime in progress. The lady behind the cash register never left her stool, but bellowed out:

"Come back here! All three of you, come here to me right now!"

There was something in her voice. Another lady I know used the same tone to me maybe a thousand times.

The trio of urchins walked to her, eyes down to the floor. The little one, the guilty one, was pushed to the front.

"I saw what you did," the lady said. "Do you know what I do to little boys who take things from me and then run away?"

The little one shook his head.

"I cut their ears off," the lady said. "You wouldn't look so good without ears, would you?"

The little one shook his head again.

31

And then he looked up at her—he was filled with terror—but she was smiling down at him now, and she said, "You're not going to do anything like that again, are you?"

And he shook his head another time and replied softly, meekly, "No, ma'am." He left the diner with his ears intact, and maybe he will never forget his rookie attempt at theft.

Most of us long gone from home forget too soon the magic of a mother's touch, be it at her table or when the need for a lesson to be learned is great.

God bless the lady behind the cash register for an occasional reminder.

Warren
Newman

*If Warren Newman had lived long enough to
have had a book published, he would have
mentioned me in it, I am sure. It's been months
since he died. Sometimes, late at night, I still
miss him hard.*

Warren Newman, for a country boy from Sanders-
ville, Georgia, was quite sophisticated. He didn't like clichés, nor
anything that was "hokey." I have put quotations around that
word, "hokey," because it was a word Warren used a great deal.

The man was an idealist, was what he was. That, and a
perfectionist.

He disliked such things as plastic flowers and neon cowboys.
What he liked were old people who sat in front of country stores,
dozing and telling good stories, dogs, and Vienna sausages eaten
directly from a can on a riverbank.

I suppose knowing all that about Warren Newman is what is
making writing this so difficult. The last thing he would have
wanted would have been—as he would have put it—"one of those
God-awful sad stories about what a great guy I was."

But here I sit on a bright Sunday morning in May writing one
of those God-awful sad stories about what a great guy he was.

Maybe the only thing I can do to temper this is to leave out a
lot of gush about how much I loved him and how much I will miss
him and just stick to the parts about how he cracked me up and
how a number of us who knew him best often wondered if he were
really from this planet.

Warren had a bizarre sense of humor, and his ideas and

33

thoughts must have come from some celestial left field where the rest of us could never reach for inspiration.

There was his Lyndon Johnson impression. He did Lyndon Johnson announcing he would not seek re-election better than Lyndon Johnson. I can still hear him—Warren, not Lyndon Johnson—pronouncing, "Mah feller Amuricahns . . . ."

There was his small-town disc-jockey voice. I think somewhere in Warren's past he had been a small-town disc jockey.

The act was a riot, and I stole it from him and I use it when I make a speech.

And there was the thing he did about a fellow getting arrested for murder down in Sandersville and what he told the authorities when they came to get him, but I couldn't come close to capturing it in print, and another thing that makes me sad is now that Warren is gone, so is that story. Forever.

What else. He was an artist. He did sketches, and they were quite good. He played guitar. He was an expert on the Civil War.

He owned a famous dog, "Springfield," the last of the long-nosed Egyptian coon hounds, which is another story.

He snored with the best of them. I shared a tent with him for seven nights on a wilderness river somewhere out in Arkansas last summer, so I ought to know.

The funny thing that happened on that trip was one morning as we started to launch our canoes, we discovered a rattlesnake in Warren's. The three adults on the trip were all afraid to remove the snake, but, luckily, there was a fifteen-year-old along who wasn't old enough to be frightened of rattlesnakes. We let him handle the situation while the three of us hid behind a tree.

One other thing. Warren Newman was a talented writer. Three years ago, he was a bartender. Then, he got a job at the newspaper helping count football contest ballots. Soon after that, he moved to some boring job on the desk. Soon after that, he became *The Atlanta Constitution's* brightest sports star. The man was moving up fast.

He would have left sports eventually, I am certain, and written of the world as he saw it. Damn, we missed something there.

Warren Newman, thirty-one, ran into a tree in his automobile Saturday morning, and he is dead. I went over to his house Saturday afternoon and petted his dog and talked to his pretty, heartbroken wife.

She told me about a short poem she had written about her husband a couple of months ago. She read it to me and said she was thinking about having it put on his gravestone. She asked me if I though it was "hokey."

Here's the poem:

> *Son of the Southland,*
> *A dreamer, kind and wise.*
> *More than most men dare imagine*
> *Shone clearly in his eyes.*

That's not "hokey." That says it. That says it all.

Dudley
Stamps

Of all the people I have met in my life, Dudley is one of them, which is the one of the nicest things anybody ever said about him.

It was great to see Dudley Stamps at my fifteenth high school reunion. It was great to see everybody, but seeing Dudley was special.

Dudley and I used to hang out together and do weird things. Actually, Dudley did weird things and I would go along to see what he was going to do next.

Dudley enjoyed driving motorized vehicles as fast as they could possibly go. The fastest I have ever traveled on land was inside the 1960 Thunderbird Dudley's parents bought him for his sixteenth birthday.

Often I questioned Dudley's parents' judgment in buying him that car, because he spent his entire junior and senior years in high school attempting suicide in this 1960 Thunderbird.

One night, the highway patrol stopped Dudley and gave him a ticket for speeding. The patrolman said he had clocked Dudley at 110 miles per hour.

Dudley was incensed. He swore he had been going at least 120.

Dudley also owned a truck. We were driving around in Dudley's truck and he said to me, "I wonder if trucks will float."

An idle thought, I figured. I figured wrong. Dudley was a man of action. He immediately drove his truck into the middle of White Oak Creek.

I learned a lot of important things hanging out with Dudley Stamps. One thing I learned is trucks won't float.

Dudley also enjoyed climbing. He would climb anything that wouldn't climb him first, like forest ranger towers, water towers, statues on the town square in the middle of the night, etc.

I was in the front seat, and Dudley was driving. We passed a tall water tower. Dudley stopped his car and attacked the water tower. I remained in the car where it was safe. It was never safe around Dudley.

Soon, I began to hear large objects crashing onto the top of Dudley's car.

Dudley had filled his pockets with large rocks before he climbed the water tower. He thought it great sport to frighten me by dropping large rocks onto the top of his car.

When Dudley eventually traded his car, for a case of beer and several back issues of *Guns* magazine, it looked like it had been through the Third Punic War.

The best fist fight I ever saw involved Dudley Stamps. It was the heavyweight championship of the ninth grade, between Dudley and the school bully.

The school bully was a dummy. He verbally assaulted Dudley one afternoon in study hall when the teacher went out of the room.

It was a close fight; but the judges, one of the tenth grade girls and myself, gave Dudley the decision. Soon afterwards, the school bully joined the drama club.

About half the class turned out for the reunion. We had a picnic in the afternoon and a dance at the Elks Club that night. They played the old songs.

We also gave out awards. I won most divorces. One of the people who helped me win that award was there. I don't mind admitting it. She looked terrific.

37

A couple of my classmates are now lawyers. One is president of a company. The girls who were pretty in high school still are.

I was proud of myself because several of my classmates walked up to me and said they read what I write in the newspaper. Some even mentioned they enjoy it.

I imagined Dudley as a hired gun. Or at least a steeplejack. He's married and has a child. He farms a little and repairs Volkswagens, he said.

We had a brief conversation.

"I see your ugly picture in the newspaper sometimes," Dudley said to me.

"Oh, yeah?"

"Yeah. But I don't read the garbage," he continued.

"Oh, no?"

"No. And the only time I see your picture is when I need some paper to put under a car so it won't leak oil on my garage floor. I look down and say, 'There's that damn fool with oil all over his stupid face.'"

Thanks, Dudley. I needed that.

"Flash"
Noles

Since LeRoy "Flash" Noles died, incidentally,
The Atlanta Constitution *has been struggling to*
right itself. The jury is still out as to whether
we will make it without him.

the funeral is over now, and LeRoy "Flash" Noles, celebrated copyboy of *The Atlanta Constitution*, has been put to rest on a day hung with mist and pall, an appropriate day for a funeral, as if there can be such a thing.

Flash died Saturday. Somebody said he had a heart attack. He was sixty-three. He had worked here for forty-two years. His "office"—a supply room marked, simply, "Flash"—was next to my own.

Flash never married, but he had a good dog once. His aunt cried on the front pew of the funeral home chapel.

What the man did for an honest living was carry newspapers and good cheer throughout the building at 72 Marietta Street.

We talked a lot. Flash enjoyed fishing. Once, he showed me a picture of himself holding a mess of catfish.

"Them things are the devil to clean," he said, "but they make good eatin'."

I will remember him. Floppy hat, boots, a limp. Over lunch after the funeral, they were saying how he thought Conway Twitty hung the musical moon.

The newspaper sent Flash away in style. His obit made page one of a section front in Sunday's paper. They even ran his picture.

Columns and editorials followed.

"I think I'm going to do something on Flash for tomorrow," I was saying.

"Not much left to say," a co-worker replied.

"I'm going to do something anyway," I said.

Flash never wrote a line of copy for *The Constitution*. He never made an editorial decision, never took a picture, never wrote a headline.

But to anyone looking around at the funeral, his importance could not be doubted. The biggies were there, publisher, editor, managing editors, and their assistants. A columnist also came and wondered if he would have drawn the same heavy crowd.

And if Flash Noles' death accomplished anything, it at least brought those of us who cover a rather hectic and complicated world, and grow cynical from the effort, into contact with an element of simplicity some of us had forgotten, and many of us had likely never known. Flash had a country funeral. There is no other description, that is the only description. The last country funeral I saw was the one they gave for my grandfather in a hot Head County church twenty years ago.

The organ was playing softly, tenderly. It was playing selections from a brown Cokesbury hymnal of my youth.

"In the Sweet By and By" was one selection. "I Love to Tell the Story" was another. And then a girl wearing glasses sang "Precious Memories." How they linger. A woman across the aisle from me dabbed at her eyes with a crumpled tissue. The women always bring crumpled tissues to a country funeral.

The preacher wore his best suit, three pieces of blue that were snug. He read the twenty-third Psalm.

He preached a "warning" service. A "warning" service is where the preacher looks down at the casket and says we're all going to be in the same shape one of these days, and we'd better get ready. Or else.

It's the "or else" part that spooks me, but truth is normally frightening. At a country funeral, they figure nothing more can be done for the dead, so let the living take heed.

That's about it. If there is a deeper message, I frankly don't feel like searching for it. Just a couple of more things.

One, the only bad thing I ever knew Flash to do was occasionally cuss a slow elevator, but that is certainly a forgivable sin, so I'm not concerned about his address in the hereafter.

Two, I just figured out why I went ahead and wrote this anyway. I wanted the late, great LeRoy "Flash" Noles, forty-two years at his post, to have something to do with one more edition of *The Atlanta Constitution*.

Courage
in the
Pulpit

*Good news. Some months after I wrote this, the
preacher and his wife decided to give it another
try.*

it is one of those big downtown churches—a "rich folks'
church," they would have called it back home.

There are a couple of assistant preachers who handle the
preliminaries at the Sunday morning service, and then the head
preacher delivers his message through a microphone. A radio
station carries it out to the "shut-ins," a good church word you
may or may not remember.

All the preachers wear long robes and have important-
sounding degrees, and the choir sings difficult arrangements you
can't tap a toe to, and people around you would probably look at
you funny if you did.

There is carpet and there are expensive windows, and you
feel like the Lord *expects* something more than a few loose coins
when they come around with the collection plate.

I have been there in the congregation a few Sundays, and
despite all the "luxury," for the lack of a better term, the fellow
worshipers are friendly and the head preacher, when he finally
takes command, is a bright and forceful man who sprinkles his
sermons with humor.

I have always liked a preacher with a sense of humor. So
many of them seem never to take off their funeral faces.

42

I don't see the need to be specific here, as far as the name of the church or the name of the head preacher, the man who can smile and fan a hell-fire at the same time.

It could happen to anybody. But when it happens to a preacher in a big church with fancy windows, tongues wag and eyebrows are lifted and you hear people saying, "What is the world coming to?"

The preacher's wife left him a few weeks ago. That happens to lawyers and doctors and insurance salesmen and ditch-diggers and newspaper columnists, but it doesn't happen to preachers because they know all the answers, and the good they do, you figure, protects them from such.

A shock wave went through the church.

"I always thought they looked so happy together," somebody said.

"You can never tell about things like that," said somebody else.

The preacher offered to resign. Could he continue to be effective with this wart on his face?

Good for the church. Sure, there was gossip, but the resignation wasn't accepted. Had it been, I would never have gone back. Not that I'm a regular or serve on committees, but I hate snootiness in any form.

It would have been *snooty* to let the man walk away. It would also have been cruel.

The preacher took some time off to put his life back in order, if that is possible, which it is not. He wrote a letter to every member of the church. Attached to his letter was a letter from his wife.

"Being a minister's wife," the gist of her explanations for the breakup went, "is very difficult. I can't handle it."

That's her business. His letter asked for understanding and prayers. Yes, there were children involved.

He came back to the pulpit last week. I caught him on the radio. Those who were there said he looked a little drained, but that he handled himself well.

That's an understatement. "Today," he said, "I have to go public with a private disaster in my own life." Few things are more difficult.

I felt for him throughout the sermon. He quoted scripture—Psalms, I think—and he asked for more understanding, and he said, "I know you have been praying for me already . . . I can feel them working."

I could sense his embarrassment, his "gnawing pain" as he put it. At the end of the sermon, he even called for others with similar problems to meet him at the altar afterwards for some safety-in-numbers reassurance.

Give him credit. Looking out on that sea of curious faces Sunday morning, he must have recalled a familiar lament that never has an answer—"Why me, Lord?"

Or maybe it does have an answer. Why you, preacher? Because you are only human.

Your flock will forget that occasionally. For your own peace of mind, don't you.

Preacher Jackson

Wayne Jackson did everything he could to keep my father from the devil in the bottle.

What made me think to look up Preacher Jackson after all these years was the news about Billy Carter that came on the heels of the news about Herman Talmadge.

Billy Carter, the president's brother, and Herman Talmadge, the millionaire United States senator from Georgia, are both now admitted alcoholics.

Talmadge was recently released from the Long Beach Naval Hospital in California, where they treat people with drinking problems. Billy Carter checked in this week.

Not just anybody can get help at Long Beach, but neither Talmadge nor Carter had any problems. The Secretary of the Navy intervened in Billy's behalf. Both men are obviously capable of paying the $266-a-day rate.

Long Beach is sort of the Hilton of rehabilitation centers. Betty Ford got help there once for a pill problem. Talmadge emerged after five weeks, went the news reports, looking "tan and fit."

Billy Carter, said the Nashville agent, will come out "a new man." Good luck. Alcoholism is a bear to whip.

Preacher Jackson knows that better than anybody. He's been at the business of trying to help people give up booze for sixteen years out in the sticks at a place called Hope Haven near Jefferson, Georgia.

"When you do what I do," he told me Wednesday, "frustration becomes a way of life."

Preacher Jackson is fifty-three. His first name is Wayne. He's a God-fearing Baptist, and he started Hope Haven in 1963. He had two bucks in his pocket.

He renovated an old school building and opened the doors to any man who would voluntarily submit to what he calls "Christian rehabilitation."

He uses no fancy drugs. He doesn't have any. There is no place to get a suntan. There are no jogging tracks.

"We don't have any carpet on the floor," he said, "because we can't afford it. We operate on faith." That means donations.

I asked him how many men come to him and leave with their drinking problem licked.

"The percentage is very, very low," he said. "I've had maybe 1,400—1,500 men come through here. If you keep a man sober for a day, you've helped him.

"But completely rehabilitated? Maybe 2 percent. The odds are just too high."

I first met Preacher Jackson—that's what everybody calls him—maybe ten or twelve years ago when I went to visit a patient of his, a man the preacher remembered well.

"How could we ever forget him?" he laughed.

"I retrieved him out of a lot of hotel rooms," he said. "and I spent a lot of time with him over the years. He'd come in with bleary eyes and needing a shave. Then, he'd hit the showers.

"He'd find a clean shirt somewhere, and get somebody to press his pants. He always wanted a crease in them. Then, he'd look for a bow tie. He always wore bow ties.

"Next thing you knew, he'd walk out looking like a million. He used to really liven this place up, too.

"We had a singing group here one time, and he joined them on the piano. I'll never forget it. He started playing 'When the

46

Saints Go Marching In,' and about the third time around, he had everybody jumping up and down.

"We don't know exactly what made him drink. He lived in a fantasy world, I think, and he had some strong guilt about something.

"We used to get a lot of calls from him when things were going bad. He'd call and tell us how much he loved us. I used to say, 'Why don't you tell us that when you're sober?' "

I said the same thing to him a thousand times.

The man Preacher Jackson and I were remembering was one of the 98 per cent who couldn't overcome alcoholism. It finally killed him. He died a pauper. "What a waste of talent," said the preacher.

Yeah, and I wonder sometimes if it could have been salvaged in a swanky place like Long Beach.

Probably not. And what's the use of such speculation? Rich people and famous people who have drinking problems are called "alcoholics." The others are called "drunks."

I should count my blessings. A drunk I loved a great deal got the best help money couldn't buy from Wayne Jackson and Hope Haven, and I should never have waited this long to thank them for their efforts.

A
Dying
Man

August 12, 1970, Claxton, Georgia. The devil in the bottle, and perhaps a thousand more that inevitably hound a fallen hero, finally won the battle.

tClaxton, Ga.

here are scenes that will never leave you. One such, for me, took place here ten years ago in little Claxton, where they make fruitcakes. Ten years. I can't believe it has been that long.

It was an August morning, hot and damp outside. I stood inside a tiny hospital room where a fifty-eight-year-old man was near death.

Around me stood a few others who also cared about him, too. One was a preacher. As the end neared, the preacher asked that we all bow our heads, and he prayed.

He asked the Lord to take the soul about to depart the ravaged body on the bed. I said a prayer of my own. I asked the Lord to ignore the preacher and leave the soul where it was.

That was the only miracle I have ever prayed for. I wasn't ready to give the man up just yet, and, frankly, I thought the preacher was rushing things a bit.

I had never seen anybody die before, I envisioned death rattles and twitching and gasping and one final heave of breath, and then the last hold of air rushing out.

It was nothing like that. The man, who was unconscious, breathed, and then he wasn't breathing anymore.

48

So much for my miracle.

The preacher asked that we bow our heads again, and we did, and he prayed again, but I forget about what this time.

I wanted to say something dramatic when he had finished, something befitting the life we had just seen pass. I said something stupid, instead. I said, "He hated hot weather, you know."

The only comfort I could find in the moment was that the man wouldn't have to live through the oppressive Georgia heat the afternoon was certain to offer. He was a big man, a fat man, and the heat was always his dreaded enemy, I recalled. You think of the strangest things at times like those.

I had held his hand during the final minutes, and I will always be thankful for that. I have often wondered since if, somewhere in his fleeting subconscious, he had known I was there.

Probably not, but it is a fantasy worth keeping. He was alone a great deal during his life, which was the real cause of his death, and I will always hope he had some faint knowledge of the fact that there was an audience for the last act he performed.

How he happened to die here, in this outpost, is still somewhat of a mystery to me. Better, I thought then and I think now, years before on a battlefield of some historic worth.

Seven of his fifty-eight years had been devoted to combat, and he had distinguished himself and had inspired others, I have heard. Better he had gone in the midst of some heroic adventure, even at a much younger age, than here between white hospital sheets.

He had found nothing but unhappiness since his last war, Korea, and he had wandered alone and lost. He was just passing through this, his last stop, when some vital organ stopped its function.

The nurse came in. Then the doctor, who noted the time before he pulled the sheet over the man's blue face.

Later, someone handed me his earthly belongings in a plastic bag. It was a small bag. Inside were shoes, socks, underwear, trousers, a shirt, an empty wallet, an old watch, and a cheap ring. Fifty-eight years, and they can put what is left of you in a small plastic bag.

I was just passing through here the other day myself, but there was time, as I drove away, to put the scene back together again. I owe the man that much—to ponder occasionally how his end had come.

I owe him a lot more than that. He's the one who gave me this name, for one thing. For another, he left me with a stockpile of stories, some of which are even true, that keep a roof over my head.

3

Great Issues

Sports Cars:
Pro and
Mostly Con

*If you are currently thinking of buying a sports
car, read this. Afterwards, if you still want to
buy a sports car, you deserve one.*

Sooner or later, everybody goes through the stage of
wanting to own a sports car. I think it has something to do with
being deprived as a child.

I had plenty to eat as a child, and I was warm at night. But I
never had the real necessities, like a trip to Europe after high
school graduation or a sports car.

I have owned all sorts of cars. My first car was a
red-and-white 1956 Chevrolet. Tennis racquets cost more today
than I paid for my first car.

I have also owned a Volkswagen, several Pontiacs and a
Vega. Of all the cars I have owned, the Vega is the one I have
never forgiven.

It was brown and hard to crank. I used to park it in bad
neighborhoods and leave the keys on the hood, hoping somebody
would steal it.

Somebody tried once. I was hiding in a nearby alley
watching with a pair of jumper cables just in case. When the Vega

wouldn't crank, I appeared with the jumper cables and offered my services to the thief.

"Forget it," he said. I gave him taxi fare home for his efforts and called a tow truck.

I finally got rid of my Vega by giving it to my ex-wife. I am a bad person.

A year-and-a-half ago, I decided it was time I had my first sports car. The eagle inside me cried for the opportunity to soar.

Get the picture:

The open road lies ahead, begging to be conquered. I wind my way along it, two steady, gloved hands sure upon the wheel of my classic new sports car. The sleek lines are unmistakable. The perfectly balanced hum of the engine is a purr.

I pass through Barletta as a streaking blur. And on through Trani, Bisceglie, Molfetta, toward Monopoli, along the Italian shore, the blue waters of the Adriatic shimmering in the sun.

My road hat sits deftly upon my head, tilted at precisely the correct, cocksure angle. My scarf treads the breeze behind me. As the road straightens, I press the toe of my right Gucci against the accelerator, and the naked eye cannot still the motion I command.

The woman beside me? A long and most unbelievable story, my friend. It began only a fortnight ago as I stood on the balcony of my hotel room in Roma . . . .

Picture that in a brown Vega that won't crank and has a lot of empty beer cans in the hatchback.

The sports car I finally bought is a British import, one of those sexy little numbers with the racing stripes and plaid seat covers. The man who sold it to me is from Tupelo, Mississippi, and chews gum. His leisure suit matched the seat covers of the car.

"Sassy chassis, ain't it?" he remarked as we looked at the car. Somehow, I thought buying a sports car would be like shopping for rare art treasures. It ain't.

I am now an expert on sports cars because I have owned one for a year-and-a-half.

Here are the advantages of owning sports cars:

1. They're cute.

Here are the disadvantages of owning sports cars:

1. Sitting in a shoebox is more comfortable.

2. Try finding somebody to work on one on a hot Sunday afternoon in Cooper, Texas.

3. While riding with the top down it is impossible to talk, smoke, listen to the radio, or keep the part in your hair. Also, bugs occasionally fly into your mouth at sixty miles per hour.

4. A lot of silly teenage girls have one, too.

5. If you hit a trailer truck head-on in a sports car, they'd be lucky to find all your movable parts in a week, despite a three-county search.

What I am trying to say here is I have passed through my sports car stage, and it was a miserable experience. The latest bad thing to happen was Tuesday morning. I was backing out of my driveway, and the steering wheel broke off the column.

Luckily, the car came to a halt against a large tree. I don't know where the steering wheel finally landed.

And in order to leave this with a clear conscience, I must also admit I never drove along the Italian coast or the shimmering Adriatic.

I made all that up on the way to work today. My neighbor's cleaning woman gave me a ride in her Vega.

The High
Price of
Ice Cream

Some of you may not think seventy-five cents for one scoop of ice cream is outrageous. So if you're that spiffy, what are you doing reading a book like this?

i read about inflation and recession and depression and the portents of economic doom that are hanging over our heads like vultures. I read about the plight of the American consumer and his never-ending battle to make ends meet.

I imagine a nation on its collective way to the poorhouse. Hitchhiking. Who can afford gasoline?

And then I pick up a copy of *Newsweek* magazine and read about people gladly paying seventy-five cents for one scoop of ice cream.

Seventy-five cents for ONE scoop of ice cream.

Hard times is when people start adding water to the soup. NOT when they can still pay seventy-five cents for one scoop of ice cream.

Newsweek reports a boom in the sales of premium-quality, top-priced ice cream in the country. Ice cream like New York's Haagen-Dazs, which sounds Dutch, carries a Scandinavian label, and is made in New Jersey.

Haagen-Dazs costs seventy-five cents a scoop, and get this, $3.50 for a quart.

"If it's good," the magazine quotes a Haagen-Dazs freak as saying, "I'll buy it."

56

So buy it. Haagen-Dazs is described as rich-and-creamy and naturally flavored. But should you EAT it? It seems a wiser investment to WEAR it instead, like on your tie or on the front of your shirt to upgrade your wardrobe.

You are dealing with an ice cream expert here, a man who has consumed gobs and gobs of it, who lusts for it and dreams about it, but a man who thinks seventy-five cents for a single scoop of ice cream is outrageous.

We didn't need a top-of-the-line, state-of-the-art, better ice cream. Ice cream was fine the way it was.

The trouble actually began with all the new flavors introduced by people like Baskin-Robbins. What was wrong with your basic vanilla, chocolate, and strawberry?

I am, and always have been, a vanilla person, myself. One of those sex guides for the sensuous woman mentioned that men who eat vanilla ice cream usually make love the same way. Plain, Jane. I won't go into what the book said about a man who prefers tutti-frutti.

Now, we have ice cream flavors like butterscotch brandy, creamy caramel, rum raisin, and even ice cream that tastes like coffee, and bubble gum.

But don't get me wrong. I'm not a total straight arrow when it comes to ice cream. I have, shall we say, "experimented" with ice cream in its more exotic forms.

Ice cream sandwiches, for instance. An occasional ice cream sandwich is harmless, but the cake-like outer covering will stick to the roof of your mouth, and it takes two Big Orange bellywashers to loosen its grip.

Fudgesicles. I've done fudgesicles. Once at a party somebody had some groovy "dreamsicles," fruit-flavored ice cream on a stick. The danger there, of course, is where might it lead? Dreamsicles today. Eskimo Pies tomorrow?

57

The best, and safest, way to eat ice cream is out of a cup, with a spoon. Cones are messy, and they taste like wet plywood.

I would like to see the return of individual cups of ice cream like they sold for a nickel when I was a kid, the ones with pictures of movie stars on the underside of the lids.

Lick the ice cream off the underside of the lid, and there was a picture of Victor Mature, or maybe even Dorothy Malone.

My boyhood friend and idol, Weyman C. Wannamaker, Jr., a great American, had this thing about Dorothy Malone. Once, he bought fifteen individual cups of ice cream. He got one Debra Paget, two Joseph Cottens, three Debbie Reynolds, four Victor Matures, and FIVE Dorothy Malones.

All that for what one lousy scoop of Haagen-Dazs costs today. Haagen-Dazs, Haagen-Smazs.

It's like Weyman said after he ate all that ice cream and licked all those lids for five pictures of Dorothy Malone.

"It ain't worth it."

People Who Talk to God

I received a great many nasty letters after writing the following. Anytime you mention God, I have discovered, you get a lot of nasty letters.

i have just completed reading a newspaper interview with a woman named Margaret Schroeder of Murphy, North Carolina, who has written a book about the fact she talks to God.

Everybody who believes in prayer can make that claim, of course, but Mrs. Schroeder says God talks back to her. As a matter of fact, she says that in the past ten years, God has sent her 13,000 personal messages.

Her book is entitled *Love, Acts of the Apostles*, and it costs $3.95, a rare bargain. If I were getting personal messages from God, I would write a book, too, but I would charge a sight more than $3.95 to let the rest of the world in on our conversations.

Mrs. Schroeder says her messages from God have to do with such things as the importance of loving one another, sacrifice, and eternal life.

I am not going to say I think Mrs. Schroeder is trying to pull a fast one, because I don't doubt much of anything these days. Billy Carter stopped drinking, the mayor of Chicago is a womanperson, and a baseball team from a foreign country has challenged for a spot in the World Series.

But I must admit I have always been a bit skeptical of people who say they get messages from God.

59

There was a man in my hometown who claimed to have gotten a message from God—Uncle Jake Gaines, the laziest man in town. One Sunday morning, Uncle Jake stood up in church and described his experience.

"His words were written across the sky," be began. "They said, 'Uncle Jake—go preach the gospel.' "

You never know, so they let Uncle Jake preach the morning sermon. Billy Graham he wasn't.

After the service, my grandfather took Uncle Jake aside. "I think you may have misread the message, Jake," he whispered. "You sure God didn't say, 'Go plow your corn?' "

What else bothers me about people who say they talk to God, like Mrs. Schroeder, is they never get any specific information.

One of the messages Mrs. Schroeder says God sent was, "Body is a great sounding board; it is the mystic chord struck by the mind."

If God decided to give out information to twentieth century mortals, I frankly don't think He would beat around the bush.

I honestly do not want this to come off as overt irreverence, but after reading about Mrs. Schroeder, I couldn't help making myself a list of specific questions I would like to ask, given the opportunity for two-way conversation with the Almighty:

What REALLY happened at Chappaquiddick? It's urgent.

How long before you do something about Howard Cosell?

Is disco a sin?

Is there life after gasoline?

Has Anita Bryant become a total embarrassment?

Did Elvis go to heaven?

Can rabbits swim?

Is Oral Roberts on the level?

Does the name "Margaret Schroeder" ring a bell?

Are Cheerleaders Really Necessary?

Of course, cheerleaders aren't necessary, but we keep them around anyway. They're the parsley of athletic competition.

ast football season, I wrote a column in which I implied cheerleaders are a waste of everybody's time. I received a great deal of mail about the column:

"You are a jerk!"—Pipsie McQueen, Farrah Fawcett High, Kilgore, Texas.

"Go blow your nose!"—Precious Sweeney, University of Arkansas at Stuttgart.

"May Tony Dorsett run over your face."—Phyllis G. Brown, Kentucky.

I frankly didn't realize people felt that strongly about cheerleaders, so I attempted to enter this season with an open mind.

Say something nice about cheerleaders for a change, I reminded myself. OK. They don't perspire as much as the players.

But that is as far as I can go. This season, I have attended both professional and college games, and I would be untruthful if I said my stance on cheerleaders has changed.

It has not. They are still a waste of time.

One, cheerleaders don't really lead cheers, because most of the people who go to football games are either too involved in beating the point spread or too bombed to pay attention to them.

Two, cheerleaders usually have silly names. Like "Pipsie" and "Precious."

Three, cheerleaders, especially at professional games, do little more than wiggle their navels for a couple of hours.

Four, most cheers are stupid:

> *Wiggle your navel left!*
> *Wiggle your navel right!*
> *Wiggle your navel up and down!*
> *And fight! Fight! Fight!*

Pressed, I suppose I can abide a cheerleader or two at college games because sis-boom-bah is part of the appeal of the collegiate game, and there needs to be somebody around who remembers the words to the alma mater.

But I would like to put all professional cheerleaders on a permanent taxi squad. Autumn Sunday afternoons have become one big pompom shaking in the face of America. There are exceptions to everything, of course; but, basically, when you have seen one shaking pompom, you have seen them all.

I blame the Dallas Cowboys for this. There was a time when professional football teams wouldn't even think of allowing a group of women to stand around in their underpants on the sidelines and bump and grind for four quarters.

But later came National Football League expansion, and a team was placed in Dallas, where the men spend a lot of time out on the range with their cattle.

Spend enough time out on the range with your cattle, and football won't be enough to occupy your mind totally on the weekends either, Tex.

That's how the Dallas Cowboys Cheerleaders came to be. Watch the game, watch the girls, too, and get along, little dogie.

Soon, practically every team in the league had its cheerleaders, with the notable exception of the Pittsburgh

Steelers, who said, "We're here to play football. Get them broads off the sidelines." The Steelers, incidentally, are Super Bowl champions.

Before the letters start to pour in again, let me offer my assurance that this column was not written from a sexist point of view.

I don't like boy cheerleaders, either. Sometimes, you see boy cheerleaders at college games. What bothers me is, what will boy cheerleaders tell their sons when they ask, "What did you do in the Big Game, daddy?"

And they will be forced to answer, "I jumped around like an idiot and screamed my fool head off."

I am even more concerned about boy baton twirlers, but that is another story entirely.

The Old
Chinchilla
Game

*All you've ever wanted to know about why NOT
to invest in chinchillas, which have an alarming
tendency to go bald.*

What I knew about chinchillas, furry little animals
that sometimes wind up as expensive coats, you could have put on
the tip end of a chinchilla's tail, only I didn't even know if
chinchillas have tails. (Later, I was to discover they most certainly
do.)

What aroused my interest in chinchillas was an advertisement that ran in the newspaper last week.

"Own Your Own Business," said the advertisement.
"Opportunity to Earn $30,000 Raising Chinchillas. Start in a
spare room, garage, basement, outbuilding, etc."

The company that placed the advertisement was International Furriers Ltd.

I could use the thirty big ones, and I have a spare room. Also,
there was a picture of a chinchilla included in the advertisement.
Chinchillas are cute little boogers.

I talked to a Mr. Flowers of International Furriers Ltd. He
became angry and defensive when I told him I worked for the
newspaper. I don't think he believed I was serious about wanting
to learn about chinchillas so I could possibly go into business
raising them.

I think he thought I was trying to stir up trouble just because a few thousand people get ripped off in chinchilla-raising schemes every year.

Mr. Flowers assured me his company would never knowingly fleece a customer. He said people who go into chinchilla-raising and lose their shirts are just dummies who do not give their animals the proper care and handling.

After he settled down a bit, I was able to get even more vital information about chinchillas.

He said chinchillas were originally from South America, but now they all live in cages in spare rooms, garages, basements, outbuildings, etc.

He said they are nocturnal animals of the rodent family. They are about the size of rabbits, he went on, and it costs a penny a day to feed one chinchilla on Ralston-Purina Chinchilla Chow.

"Do they have tails?" I asked.

"They most certainly do," Mr. Flowers assured me.

He also said he would sell six chinchillas—one boy and five girls—for $3,400 and he would even throw in the cages.

I also wanted to know how much a ready-for-market chinchilla is worth and how many people are actually making $30,000, but that's where Mr. Flowers became testy again and I decided it would be best to hang up.

What I did next was call the Governor's Office of Consumer Affairs, to ask would it be smart for a person to get involved in raising chinchillas.

Not by the hair of your chinny chinchilla, said a spokesperson. Here's why:

1. Contrary to what a chinchilla salesman might tell you, chinchillas are NOT easy to raise. They are subject to a variety of diseases, traumas, and even emotional breakdowns which affect their breeding habits and the quality of their offspring. There is nothing worse than a chinchilla gone bonkers.

2. Chinchillas make a lot of noise at night. They're

nocturnal, remember? Unfortunately, most of the suckers who get involved in raising them aren't.

3. Sometimes, chinchillas lose all their hair. A bald chinchilla is a worthless chinchilla.

4. Sometimes, even worse things happen. Sometimes, they gnaw their feet off.

5. Chinchilla salesmen often claim chinchillas reproduce three times a year. That's a bunch of Chinchilla Chow.

6. Spare rooms, garages, basements, outbuildings, etc., are NOT conducive to raising chinchillas. A New York chinchilla scam recently had people trying to raise chinchillas in their bedrooms. They are the same people who keep Florida swampland salesmen in business.

7. Companies that put people in the chinchilla business have a tendency to move around a lot.

8. Most chinchilla buying and selling is done through large associations. And the chinchilla market right now is lousy.

I wanted this to be a thorough investigation, so I also looked for somebody who has actually had a chinchilla-raising experience. I found somebody.

His name is Bill Paulidis and he is a furrier for S. Baum and Co., an Atlanta firm.

Mr. Paulidis once tried to raise chinchillas on Ponce de Leon Avenue. He had 180 of them. They all got sick and lost their hair. In one night, Mr. Paulidis had to put thirty-nine chinchillas out of their misery.

He lost $25,000.

"Anybody who puts money into chinchillas," said Mr. Paulidis, "is crazy."

End of investigation.

Me
and
My Guccis

*Sometime later, someone stole the very pair of Guccis
I am writing about here. I left them in the locker
room of where I play tennis, and when I returned,
they were gone, which made me feel very good. At
least one person I hang around with at the tennis
courts has some class. I never would have guessed it.*

all my adult life, I have attempted to rise above my humble beginnings. Take shoes, for example. Now that I have steady work and live in the city, I like to wear nice shoes.

In the boondocks, we didn't wear shoes unless it was an absolute necessity. Like your feet would freeze if you didn't, or there was a funeral.

My boyhood friend and idol, Weyman C. Wannamaker, Jr., a great American, didn't wear shoes even on those occasions, but he did wash his feet twice a week whether they needed it or not.

The first time I saw Weyman in a pair of shoes they were forced upon him.

We were in the sixth grade, and the teacher organized a field trip to Atlanta to hear a performance by the symphony orchestra. As the bus pulled away from the school, she noticed Weyman was barefooted.

Horrified, she ordered the bus driver to stop at the nearest shoe store, where she bought Weyman a pair of shoes. He protested, but the teacher hit him in the mouth and Weyman didn't mention the shoes again.

67

During the performance of the symphony orchestra, however, Weyman's feet began hurting him, so he took off his shoes and hung his bare feet over the railing of the balcony. Unfortunately, he was between washes.

The entire percussion section and two flute players stopped in the middle of Chopin's Movement No. 5 to search for what had obviously passed away days earlier.

I always think of Weyman when I pull on a new pair of shoes. Lately, some of the fellows down at the lodge have been giving me the business because I now own a pair of stylish loafers by Gucci, the famous Italian leatherperson.

I prefer to think their boorish, catty remarks stem from ignorance, sprinkled with at least a tad of jealousy.

"I knew him," said one of the buzzbrains, wearing a pair of hideous lace-ups named for something you eat with fried catfish, "when he wore high-top tennis shoes and ran rabbits."

How utterly crude. And untrue. I wore low-cuts.

My new Guccis were a gift from a lady friend who brought them back from Palm Beach, where they have a Gucci store. They don't have Gucci stores except in spiffy places like Palm Beach. It's easier to move an NFL expansion franchise team into town.

My lady friend is always bringing me nice gifts when she goes on trips. Once she went to the drugstore and brought me a giant bottle of mouthwash and some extra-strength Tegrin shampoo.

I must do something nice for her. Maybe I'll take her bowling.

What makes a pair of stylish Italian loafers by Gucci so appealing is their softness, their master workmanship, and their price.

I've bought cars for less. Walk into a Gucci store, and they ask for your shoe size second. First, they want a quick glance at your Dun and Bradstreet.

Not just anybody can wear a pair of Gucci shoes, of course. Those crass dolts down at the lodge, for instance.

"You get a purse, too?" cracked one of the sorry lot, a hint of white socklet peering outside the top of his brogans.

Disgusting.

My new Guccis are an unpretentious oxblood, accented perfectly with buckles and slightly raised heels.

The cushioned inner soles wear the proud Gucci crest with the subtle, but effective announcement, "Made in Italy," as if there were any doubt.

When I am in the company of individuals with the proper breeding to appreciate such hallmarks of style, I am not hesitant to remove one of my new shoes to prove I am wearing the Real McCoy.

"Have you noticed I am wearing Guccis?" I asked the hostess at a dinner party.

"Frankly, I haven't," she said.

I took off one of my shoes and showed her the proud Gucci crest on the cushioned inner soles. I didn't want to stay at her stupid dinner party anyway.

I also called Weyman C. Wannamaker, Jr., back home and told him I am now wearing Guccis. I knew he would be proud.

"You wearing them shoes," he said, "is like putting perfume on a hog."

My Kind
of Beauty
Queen

. . . And whatever happened to Barbi Benton?

the wires carried an interesting interview the other day with the newly-crowned Miss Universe, an eighteen-year-old from Venezuela.

I take that back. It was not an interesting interview at all. As a matter of fact, it was a very dull interview, because it was like every other interview with beauty queens.

Beauty queens today have a thing about denying they are sex objects. That's nothing. So do girls who pose with no clothes on in magazines.

Open a magazine and pull out the centerfold, and there is the Lustlady of the Year revealing everything but her shoe size.

"I can't stand a man who wants me only for my body," she is saying in the caption. "I have a brain, too, and I can use it. I know six state capitals and once I went to a museum."

If I've read where one beauty queen was saying there is more to her than what she has managed to stuff inside her tight-fitting swimsuit, I've read where a thousand more were making the same irrelevant remarks.

If brains were all that important in a beauty contest, you could enter wearing a Hefty Bag.

The current Miss Universe is Maritza Sayalero. She is from Caracas. Her father is an engineer, which has nothing to do with anything but is the kind of incidental information they put in interviews with beauty queens to help fill up space.

Maritza was posing for tourists in New York City in her tight-fitting swimsuit in front of the statue of Prometheus at Rockefeller Center, and, sure enough, some reporter asked her if she considered herself a sex symbol.

And, sure enough, Miss Universe wiggled and giggled and said, "Even though I am beautiful, I don't consider myself a sex symbol."

Even though she is beautiful, what does she consider herself? Posing at Rockefeller Center in her tight-fitting swimsuit, one of those eye-poppers with slits down the sides, she was no sack of potatoes, por favor.

The interview also carried information concerning Miss Universe's plans for when her reign is over and she returns to Caracas.

She wants to be an architect.

"I want to design beautiful buildings," she said, "but with a purpose—for the poor."

I am sure the poor people in Caracas will appreciate that. Give them a few beautiful buildings and maybe they will quit complaining about being cold and hungry.

Give me a beauty queen who understands the rules of the game. Give me a beauty queen like Kathy Sue Loudermilk, who won the coveted Miss Collard Festival Queen title seven years running back home, breaking Cordie Mae Poovy's string of four in a row.

That's not the only string Kathy Sue broke. When the one that held up the top of her swimsuit snapped, that's how she ousted Cordie Mae in the first place.

Kathy Sue Loudermilk knew what a beauty contest was all about. Every year, she ordered a new swimsuit from the Sears catalog and every year, she was living proof that you could, in fact, stuff one hundred pounds of collards into a fifty-pound sack if you squeezed and packed and pushed long and hard enough.

Even the Baptist preacher always turned out to watch Kathy Sue in action at the pageant. Once, he even allowed himself a bellowing, "Hallelujah!" when Kathy Sue, sensing she might be in trouble with the judges for missing a question concerning the current price of hog vaccine, gave a couple of quick hip-flips to make up the lost points.

The county seat newspaper always dispatched a photographer and a reporter to cover the festival, and one year they posed Kathy Sue in her swimsuit on a tractor.

The reporter asked, "Miss Loudermilk, do you consider yourself a sex symbol?"

Kathy Sue never blinked.

"Does a duck have lips, Four-Eyes?" she replied as she cranked the John Deere, did a quick wheelie and disappeared down a dirt road.

I said it then, and I will say it now: "There goes my kind of beauty queen."

A Hero Unmasked

Do cowboys ever cry? Sure, even the Lone Ranger . . .

i spent an entire afternoon and part of an evening trying to reach the Lone Ranger on the telephone. You don't just pick up the telephone and ask information for the number of the Lone Ranger, but I finally resorted to that when all other efforts failed.

"I am trying to reach a Mr. Clayton Moore," I said to the operator in California. "He's the Lone Ranger."

"Is that a person or a business, sir?" she asked.

"A person," I said. "You've never heard of the Lone Ranger?"

"The rock singer?" she replied.

I hung up. Probably some mindless nineteen-year-old, high on a Hostess Twinkie.

Perhaps it was best I never reached him. What would I have said to "the masked rider of the plains"?

"Tough luck"?

"Hang in there"?

"How's Tonto"?

They stuck it to Clayton Moore, who portrayed the Lone Ranger from 1949 to 1956 on television, in a Southern California court the other day.

A judge ordered him to take off his mask and go ride off somewhere and drop dead. At least, that's what it sounded like to me.

73

I didn't understand all the legal mumbo jumbo—and I really didn't try—but the judge said Clayton Moore no longer has any claim to the role he made famous and ordered that he no longer make any public appearances wearing his mask.

They're making a new film about the legendary western hero of my youth, and the film company said Moore, who is sixty-four, is too old to play the character. They wanted him to remove his mask "to avoid confusion."

That's a lot of trail dust. Buddy Ebsen, who is certainly no tenderfoot, can still bring 'em to justice as Barnaby Jones, so why put Clayton Moore in mothballs before his time?

According to news reports, Clayton Moore cried when the judge handed down his decision. The dirty galoot.

I go all the way back to the early fifties with Clayton as the Lone Ranger and Jay Silverheels at Tonto, and Silver and Scout, who played themselves.

Merita Bread sponsored the show. "Come with us now to those thrilling days of yesteryear, . . etc."

I even remember a Lone Ranger joke. It was funny the first time I heard it, when I was ten or eleven, and it is even funnier now because Indians quit taking any grief a few years back.

The Lone Ranger and his trusty sidekick Tonto—who was always referred to as an "Injun" by badmen and other insensitive creeps on the show—were surrounded by ten million original Americans all dressed up in war paint and carrying bows and arrows and tomahawks and rifles they had borrowed from the local cavalry fort.

"Well, Tonto," says the Lone Ranger in Clayton Moore's deep, resonant voice, "it looks like we've finally come to the end of our trail."

Tonto, meanwhile, had other ideas. He replies:

"What's this 'we' business, white-eyes?"

74

Things have been tough all over for Old West television stars lately. Roy's got a bum ticker, you may have heard.

Hoppy died. Lash LaRue, the last word I had, was cracking the whip for Jesus in a tent crusade.

And now, this. A judge has taken the mask off the Lone Ranger.

Maybe if I had reached Clayton Moore on the telephone, I could have given him a message from his fans, and I know I could have spoken for all of them.

Maybe I could have said something like, "It's no big thing, *Kemo Sabe*. You're still the Lone Ranger to us, and we'll always love you."

He would have probably liked to have heard that. Especially the "we" part.

Shafting the Kids: Part I

Most of the time, the biggest trouble with young people is adults. That is what I was trying to say in the next two pieces, which are about alcohol and sex.

Sometimes I dislike being in the company of young adults. That is because sometimes they ask probing, thoughtful questions I cannot answer. I find what I do most when talking to young people is make apologies and excuses for their elders.

It will happen to me again. I will be with a group of young adults, and they will ask me why the would-be grown folks who make the laws of the state are trying to put the screws to them again.

But damned if I will hide from the truth this time. The Georgia General Assembly, which often resembles recess at the playschool, is considering depriving eighteen-year-olds—possibly even nineteen-year-olds and twenty-year-olds, too—of the right to purchase alcoholic beverages legally.

That is outrageous.

We lowered the legal drinking age from twenty-one to eighteen in this state during the Vietnam War. That was because we could no longer face ourselves knowing we could send a young man to die for no apparent reason in a war that made no apparent sense and still deprive him of a full citizenship.

But "times have changed," read an editorial last week that favored raising the drinking age again.

What on earth does that mean? That full citizenship is only valid when we are in the middle of an idiotic war? What if we get ourselves involved in another one? Times haven't changed enough that we wouldn't. And if there is a next time, guess who would get the call to duty and death again? That same eighteen-year-old the state legislature is trying to tell he must now relinquish his right to buy booze.

The state legislature giveth. I am all for that. But I personally get very nervous when any body of lawmakers or law enforcers starts trying to taketh away. Rights are not to be dangled in front of the citizenry as candy before a drooling baby.

There is, of course, the argument that because the drinking age has been lowered to eighteen, it is now easier for high school students to obtain alcohol. The proponents of lowering the drinking age point to an increase in teenage alcoholism.

Teenagers drink because they are programmed to do so by adults who can't hold any function without a cocktail beforehand. By adults like the state legislators who had a cocktail party scheduled every night of the first week of their current session.

Television, movies, and advertising—all run by adults— picture drinking as chic, as fun, as almost necessary in order to be functional within our society. Until all that is changed, teenage drinking will continue to increase, and a tub full of ridiculous regulations won't even begin to reverse the trend.

Also, I find it terribly unfair to ask an eighteen-year-old, who can vote, pay taxes, and reproduce the species, to give up his or her right because we can't convince a sixteen-year-old to wait a couple of years.

The drinking age for me was twenty-one. I had no trouble whatsoever in a town of 300, getting my hands on enough beer to turn me green when I was fifteen.

When I was eighteen, I registered, by law, for the draft, I entered college, held down a job, paid taxes, successfully proposed marriage to another eighteen-year-old, and was told I could vote.

If there was anything I wasn't ready to do yet, it was vote. One afternoon in 1964, I got blitzed at the fraternity house and went out and cast a ballot for Lyndon Johnson.

We have put the shaft to young adults long enough. We have told them one thing and meant another. We have preached to them one thing and practiced another. We have insisted they pay support to and help defend our society, but at the same time we have tried to tell them they cannot enjoy all the privileges of it.

"Bless the Beasts and the Children." It was a song from a movie of the same name. And there was the lyric: "Bless the beasts and the children/For in this world, they have no voice/They have no choice."

If the Georgia General Assembly wants to take away somebody's right to drink, then so be it.

I would be solidly in favor of a new law making it illegal for any state legislator to get himself soused in an Atlanta bar before going out looking for hookers while he was supposed to be at the business of taking care of the welfare of the citizens he represents.

Let's see a vote on that one, boys.

Shafting
the Kids:
Part II

there was no such thing as sex education when I was in school. I take that back. There was plenty of sex education in my school, but classes were conducted behind the grandstand of the baseball diamond and the teacher usually had only a couple of years on his students.

We did have "health" classes in school. That is where you learned clean fingernails are important, if you don't brush your teeth regularly your teeth will fall out, and you can get all the Vitamin D you need by spending a lot of time out in the sun.

We also had biology classes where we did hear something about sex, but only if it involved a couple of frogs.

But times changed. Educators finally began to realize that perhaps the reason so many of their female students were getting pregnant—some at ridiculous ages like twelve and thirteen—was because all they knew about sex was the basics of how to perform it.

So, gradually, sex education has been introduced into many of our schools. There has been protest, of course, because some parents and school board members still think it best for children to learn about sex in other places.

Like behind the grandstand of a baseball diamond.

Take Cobb County, for instance. They are always fighting about something in the Atlanta suburb of Cobb County. This time, it is whether to introduce a unified sex education program into the sixth, seventh, and eighth grades.

Those in favor of the program argued at a recent school board meeting that it is important because an estimated 30,000 American girls under the age of fifteen will get pregnant this year.

Those against the program had a good argument, too. Cobb County school board member John McClure said students need less sex education and more teaching of "self-respect, discipline, and patriotism."

He also suggested sex education be handled in the home.

"But not everybody has a home," countered a Cobb County high school senior who came to the meeting.

"Hmmmp!", said board member McClure, who could be suffering from chalk dust on the brain.

We think nothing of teaching our children all about wars. Half of the time I was in school, I was learning about a war, the Third Punic all the way to the Great WWII.

People get maimed and killed in wars. Sex has to do with loving. Teach 'em about war, but ignore the little brats when they ask about sex.

The new sex education plan didn't pass at the Cobb school board meeting. The vote was 3-3, but the superintendent has already said he would not ask his teachers to teach the program if the board were split on such a "controversial issue."

I don't know if this will help, but it is probably worth a try. For those Cobb students who will be deprived of sex education for at least another year, here is my own sex short-course.

Clip and save:

● Having sex, even if you are only twelve, can make babies.

● Having a baby while you are still a kid is a bummer.

● If you are determined to have sex no matter what anybody tells you, there are ways to avoid making a baby. They are called "contraceptives." Ask an older friend who won't go berserk how to obtain them.

- There is nothing dirty about sex. It is a beautiful and necessary part of life.
- Many grown people would be better off if they realized that.

The Rumored
Closing of
Harold's Barbecue

*Harold's lives on to this day. The barbecue and
the crackling cornbread are still good, the
posters about Jesus are still on the wall, and
there's still no beer.*

there is a nasty rumor going around the city that I would
like to quash immediately.

Harold's Barbecue, that wonderful haven for lovers of pork
down past Atlanta Stadium, is not going to close.

I repeat, is NOT going to close.

I first heard the nasty whisperings a couple of weeks ago
when a friend, a fellow barbecue junkie, walked into my office,
pale as a sheet.

"They can't do this!" he screamed. "I won't stand for it! I'll
write Herman Talmadge!"

Better hurry, I said, if you want to write ol' Herman.

"OK," my friend went on, "I'll write Guy Sharpe! But
somebody has to put a stop to this!"

Stop to what?

"You haven't heard?" my friend asked. "Harold's Barbecue
is selling out to a trucking company, and there are no plans to
reopen."

You could have knocked me over with a sliced sandwich,
outside meat, toast the bread.

As I have mentioned before, to my taste, there are three

great barbecue joints in Georgia. You could not rate Ruth, Gehrig, DiMaggio. Neither could you rate Harold's Barbecue in Atlanta, Sprayberry's in Newnan, and Sweat's, Soperton branch.

They are all superior places to eat barbecue, the Holy Barbecue Triumvirate, if you will.

Harold's close? Harold's is one of the reasons I went through all the trouble to escape Chicago.

I dialed the number with shaking hands. I said a little prayer. "Lord, don't let it be true."

I talked to Harold himself. Harold is Harold Hembree. His father opened Harold's Barbecue thirty-two years ago. The son has operated the business for twenty-two years.

"Harold," I began, "are you going to close?"

"Good Lord, no!" he replied.

Marvelous, absolutely marvelous.

"That rumor gets out all the time," Harold went on. "There's a trucking company close to us, and one time we talked about selling them this property.

"But they were going to give us a new place nearby and build whatever we wanted, but that never worked out.

"I have no plans to close, now or ever. I've been at this too long to try anything else."

I could go on about the quality of the barbecue at Harold's, but that would only start an argument. People feel strongly about their barbecue.

What I do want to say about Harold Hembree's establishment is it *looks* like a good barbecue joint ought to look. It's small. It's not fancy. There is no glass, no potted plants, no wicker.

The food is simple. Barbecue sandwiches, barbecue plates, chopped or sliced. Potato chips. Pickles. Brunswick stew. Cornbread. *Crackling* cornbread.

"That was mama's idea," Harold said.

Harold's is a total family operation.

83

"Counting nieces, sisters, and wives," Harold said, "there are about thirteen of us working here."

I also like the way the walls are decorated. Harold's family is serious about its religion.

"God Is My Co-Pilot." "Lean on Jesus." There are a lot of religious posters around on the walls at Harold's.

There was one other rumor I wanted to check out as long as I had Harold on the line, the one that said maybe it wouldn't be long before you could get a beer along with your barbecue at Harold's.

"No truth to that, either," he said. "Mama wouldn't stand for it."

Some things, some people endure the ravages of progress. I will sleep better tonight knowing that.

Golf, or
A Reasonable
Facsimile Thereof

Golf is the favorite game of insurance salesmen,
car thieves, and Methodist ministers. I don't
know exactly what that means, but it is
certainly worth pondering.

What's always been wrong with golf is, any way you
slice it, golf is a dull game.

The players are dull, robots carrying sticks. They don't even
spit or scratch their privates like other athletes. The spectators
are dull. They applaud even when some guntz hits a good shot.

The television announcers are dull, too. If Dave Marr cracks
you up, you probably think Bernard Kalb is a riot.

Take the United States Open golf tournament, played
somewhere near Toledo last week. Dull. A couple of players tried
to put a little life in the stodgy proceedings, but all those stuffy
United States Golf Association (USGA) officials in their
long-sleeved white shirts nearly had a hissy.

(All my life I have wanted to know the exact definition of the
word "hissy." I think it means turning red in the face and
stomping and raving around like something crazy.)

One of the players, Lon Hinkle, discovered it was closer
from tee to green on a par-five hole to hit his drive into another
fairway. To show you how dull golf is, that was front-page sports
news for days.

The USGA would have nothing of it. They ordered a tree
planted near the tee so Lon Hinkle couldn't take the scenic route.

Put the USGA in charge of sex and it would eliminate body contact.

Then there was young Bobby Clampett. Young Bobby Clampett missed the cut, but they asked him to play along the next day anyway because somebody still in the field needed a partner.

Graciously, Bobby Clampett agreed and took a busman's holiday. He also hit a few of his tee shots from his knees and joked around with the gallery.

It didn't matter Bobby Clampett's knee-shots were long and straight. It didn't matter there is nothing in the rules of golf that says you can't hit the ball from a kneeling position. And what's wrong with joking around with the gallery?

"Watch me hit this ball on my knees," said Bobby Clampett.

"Ha! Ha!" laughed the gallery.

The hilarity is killing me.

Anybody seen Bobby Clampett lately? Of course not. He was dragged away from the thirteenth hole by USGA officials and shot.

I played golf last week. I hadn't played golf in ten years. I quit because I was a lousy golfer and because I didn't like to walk around in the woods. There are spiders and snakes in there.

Also, it was making me a dull person. After a round of golf, I thought a big night out was a couple of hands of canasta with my neighbor, Mr. Forndyce. Mr. Forndyce was a nice enough fellow, but he was also eighty-three and had been declared legally dead from his eyebrows down thirty years earlier.

But I finally found a way to play golf that is fun. I played in the annual Busch Bash, formerly the Old Milwaukee Open, at the Newnan Country Club. Two grown men named Joe Lawson and Jim Mottola are in charge of it. If Joe Lawson and Jim Mottola ran the U.S. Open, Bobby Clampett could hit balls standing on his head and they wouldn't care.

The Busch Bash involves playing twenty-seven holes of golf and drinking a beer on each one. There are some terrific rules:

- If you don't want to hit the ball, you can throw it. I didn't hit the ball so well, but I made some excellent throws.
- If you don't want to hit the ball or throw it, fine. Drink another beer.
- If you hit the ball into the woods, forget it. Hit somebody's ball that didn't go into the woods.
- You can wear tennis shoes.
- Wives and girlfriends of participants are encouraged to stay away from the trailer parked behind the seventeenth green.
- The night before the tournament, there is a party from seven until nine o'clock that lasts until three in the morning.
- The night after the tournament, there is a party that still may be going.

There are always prizes at the annual Busch Bash, but tournament officials never remember to give them out. In fact, at the party after the tournament, I asked Joe Lawson who won, and he said, "Who knows?"

That's my kind of golf tournament. I only wish some officials from the USGA, the pompous old goats, could have been there. They would have had a hissy. A double.

4
Fighting City Hall

Grizzard
for
Mayor

My campaign never got off the ground. I was selling
bumper stickers for $17.50 each to raise money.
Counting the one my mother didn't buy, I didn't sell
any. Also, I got some sage political advice from one
of my readers who reminded me, "Grizzard, the only
thing you ought to run for is the city limits."

i know you are all going to fall down laughing when you read
this, but it wasn't my idea. It came from a group of dentists over at
Emory University.

They wrote me a letter that began, "Atlanta is ready for, and
in need of, responsible leadership in city government."

The understatement of the year. Our City Council is a
monkey show, at best, and our mayor—you read it here
first—was dropped on his head as a small boy, which explains
some of his delirious actions like making plans to run in a
statewide election against Senator Herman Talmadge.

Outside Atlanta, they think Maynard Jackson is the name of a
new hog vaccine.

You also have to question the mayor's recruiting abilities. He gave the city A. Reginald Eaves, remember. And he is also responsible for Tweedle-Dum and Tweedle-Dee, Brown and Napper, over at police headquarters.

Their crack leadership of the police force has the rest of us looking for places to hide, as the crime rate soars. A friend in Des Moines called the other day and said, "I was planning to come visit you in Atlanta, but now I'm not sure. Shouldn't we plan to meet somewhere safer? Like Juarez or Newark?"

The dentists over at Emory have strongly suggested that because I am always writing as if I know it all, maybe I should run for mayor of Atlanta in the upcoming 1981 election.

Pull yourselves together. It's not that damned funny. I was treasurer of my freshman class in high school, and when I was a kid, I used to shovel out what the horses left in the barn. I know a little something about politics.

(What does shoveling out what horses leave in the barn have to do with politics? I don't think I have to answer that question.)

Dr. Thomas W. McDonald has appointed himself campaign chairman of the "Grizzard for Mayor in '81 Committee," and he lists Dr. George Ulrich and Dr. George Pryles as his associates.

Their letter drafting my candidacy further stated, "Campaign strategy and meetings are under way, and an effective bumper sticker blitz has been initiated."

I must say I am flattered. "Mayor Lewis Grizzard." "Mr. Mayor Lewis Grizzard." "His Honor, Mayor Lewis Grizzard." They all have a certain ring.

But I would have some problems of my own as mayor. For one thing, I don't really need a car; and when someone else drives, it makes me nervous. And all those bodyguards scurrying around and opening my doors would make me feel a bit pompous.

I probably would do something dumb like fire my bodyguards; because I happen to think if anybody needs bodyguards in this town, it's not the mayor, it's the working stiff who has to brave the raging streets alone.

And then I would have all those fat-cat jobs to hand out, the ones you give to your pals, or former pals, like A. Reggie.

All my friends already have good jobs.

And I have no idea what to do about Central City Park, the downtown zoo. Yes, I do, but electric fencing is so expensive. I don't get free drinks at Billy's, and would that much of an outsider really have a fighting chance at getting elected?

I'll just stick here, fighting the daily battle to produce a column for a great, metropolitan newspaper. Besides, you'll have plenty of choices for a new mayor in 1981, without my getting in the way.

Statesmen like A. Reggie and Mike Lomax, who has a cute beard and knows some rock stars, will probably be in the battle. And if Leroy Johnson, the new head of the Stadium Authority, can pass out enough big cigars and free parking at Falcons games to the right people, who knows about him?

I am not now, nor will I ever be, a candidate. But collector's item "Grizzard for Mayor" bumper stickers are available. Send $17.50, or more if you can spare it, and my staff of volunteers will see that your sticker is in the mail promptly.

Sure, I'll make a few quick bucks for doing nothing. But I already told you I know a little something about politics.

Adventures of the Drug Fairy

City Councilman James Bond is one of my favorite Atlanta politicians. His tailor, incidentally, is the same guy who designed the Hefty Bag.

i called a detective in the auto theft division of the Atlanta Police Department Wednesday and promised him if he answered a few of my questions candidly, I wouldn't use his name. Sometimes such tactics are necessary in big-time journalism.

He agreed.

What would happen, I began, if I called the police emergency number, like any ordinary citizen would do, to report a theft of a radio and a tape system from my car?

"We would send over a uniformed officer," said the detective, "and he would make out a report."

What would happen, I went on, if I called the chief of police directly with such a complaint?

"You wouldn't do that," said the detective.

"But what if I did?"

"If you got through, I suppose he would just send over a uniformed officer, and he would make out a report."

There was one more question. What would happen if I were a city councilman and a member of the Public Safety Committee, which overlooks police department matters, and I called the chief with my complaint? Would I get special treatment? Would I, for instance, be sent a detective rather than a uniformed cop?

94

"I see what you mean," said the detective. "But let's face it, that kind of thing has *always* gone on, and it always will. Who do you think they would send over if Jimmy Carter called and said somebody had broken into his car?"

Good point. We take care of our own on nearly every level of government. It's an American tradition. Like Bunker Hill, remembering the *Maine*, and fixing traffic tickets.

That brings us to the recent case of Atlanta City Councilman James Bond, who just happens to be a member of the Public Safety Committee which overlooks the police department.

Somebody broke into his car and took his radio and tape system. He did not call the police emergency number. He called Chief George Napper. Who came to Bond's house to investigate? Not Charlie the Cop, but Detective R. T. Ford.

Detective Ford did a thorough job in his investigation. This wasn't Joe Doe he was dealing with, remember.

Detective Ford did too good a job. Somebody should talk to Detective Ford. Know what he found in Councilman Bond's car besides a missing radio and tape system? He found something that looked a lot like marijuana cigarettes, fellow citizens.

He found one unsmoked cigarette behind the front seat. He found nine already-smoked cigarettes in Councilman Bond's ashtray. Just to prove himself wrong of his suspicions, Detective Ford sent the substance to the Georgia Crime Lab for identification.

Holy Case Dismissed! The substance was marijuana! Marijuana is against the law! There must be an explanation!

There was. Chief Napper handled the matter himself. After all, this had been his baby from the start.

"There is no reason to believe the owner of the car had any responsibility for placing the marijuana there," said the chief, adding, "Somebody other than the owner could have placed it there."

Of course. The Drug Fairy, for one. The chief even mentioned the thief might have done it. That's logical. A thief decides to rip off Councilman Bond's car. He opens the door with a coat hanger and lies down in the seat to partake of the goodies.

While he is there, he decides to mix a little pleasure with business and smokes nine marijuana cigarettes in the minute-and-a-half it takes to dislodge Councilman Bond's radio and tape system. At least he had the courtesy to crush out all nine in the ashtray and leave one unsmoked joint behind the front seat for the next thief.

Just so nobody gets any wrong ideas, Chief Napper has assured Atlanta citizens that Councilman Bond's high position in the city government had absolutely nothing to do with his decision not to file charges against Bond.

Even the Drug Fairy wouldn't fall for that one.

A Toast
to the
Poor People

*The hero of this story is A. Reginald Eaves, who
once bought an expensive love seat for his office
when he was Atlanta's public safety commissioner,
and who likes big, chauffeur-driven limos and lots of
bodyguards and shiny suits. Isn't it sad poor people
in other parts of the country besides Atlanta don't
have a guy like A. Reginald Eaves on their side?*

in the past, when I read articles about the possibility of A.
Reginald Eaves' becoming mayor of Atlanta, I would get down on
the floor and roll around and laugh.

Stone Mountain will crumble, the Peachtree Plaza will fall
before that will happen, I would say.

My attitude changed Tuesday night. I am now convinced A.
Reggie, former public safety commissioner, current county
commissioner, and a big man in a number of local discos, could
become the next mayor of Atlanta.

How does that feel to me? How does it feel to stand around
and wait for a homemade H-bomb to go off?

A. Reggie, as you probably know, was against the idea to
raise the local sales tax. Maynard Jackson, the current Atlanta
mayor, was for it, and so was his hand-picked successor, Michael
Lomax.

The sales tax hike was soundly trounced in Tuesday's
election. Said the political experts, "The sales tax defeat showed
the strong base of support for A. Reginald Eaves."

97

A. Reggie didn't want anybody to forget that, so as soon as he could find somebody with a microphone, he started campaigning. I watched his performance on the eleven o'clock news.

"This is a great victory for the poor people," said A. Reggie. As soon as a person starts talking about great victories for the poor people, you can bet the farm he is campaigning.

A. Reggie wore a pin-striped gangster suit for the occasion and was celebrating in a hotel room with a lot of others, who may or may not have been drinking champagne out of the glasses they were holding.

I think they probably were drinking champagne, because that's what you usually drink when the poor people win one.

I will be the first to admit A. Reggie is smarter than I originally thought. I used to think he was a complete dummy. Now, I think he is only a half-dummy, which makes him one of our most intelligent local politicians.

Recall, he was fired as public safety commissioner by the mayor, the same fellow who hired him on the basis that they were old friends. It is difficult to get fired from a job where your boss is an old chum, but A. Reggie managed it.

Yet A. Reggie landed on his feet. He could have left town in disgrace. Instead, he chose to become a martyr. Martyrs have a big edge in elections, and that is how A. Reggie got elected to the county commission.

Then he started going around winning great victories for the poor people. The Falcons' playoff win over Philadelphia last season, for instance.

"Great victory for the poor people," said A. Reggie.

He gave away such jobs as personal bodyguard and chauffeur to poor people like county policemen, and when he walks into a local disco, he buys the first ten poor people to recognize him a drink.

A Toast to the Poor People

There are a number of things that bother me about the possibility of A. Reginald Eaves' becoming mayor of Atlanta:

- He forever loused up the police department when he was chief. Imagine what he could do as mayor.
- I don't think he really cares about poor people. I think he cares more about personal bodyguards and chauffeurs.

After the sales tax vote was in Tuesday night, A. Reggie also said, "The people have more intelligence than we gave them credit for."

Let's hope so. God, let's hope so.

Frontier
Mayor

It is very helpful to a newspaper columnist when the local mayor is taken to doing weird things, thus giving the newspaper columnist a topic. I would like to thank Atlanta Mayor Maynard Jackson for all his help through the years . . .

i've been sleeping much more soundly recently since I read about Mayor Maynard Jackson's one-man battle against crime in Atlanta.

We have a great deal of crime in Atlanta: murder, robbery, rape, jacking up cars on the streets.

The other day, the mayor was riding around town in his limousine. People probably said, "Look, there's Mayor Jackson riding around town in his limousine. Why isn't he back at his office trying to do something about the rising crime rate?"

That's the people for you. What the chumps don't realize is, you can't stop crime sitting behind a desk pushing a pencil.

"Frontier Mayor" Maynard Jackson wasn't just riding around town. He was on patrol.

Suddenly, he spotted a crime in progress. Not murder. Not robbery. Not rape. But *jacking cars up on the streets*. The mere sound of the words themselves is enough to make your skin crawl.

"Whoa!" shouted "Frontier Mayor" Maynard to his limo driver. Disregarding his own safety, the mayor leaped from the limo, opening his own door in the process, and marched right into J. K. Ramey's tire store on Walton Street.

100

Out front of J. K. Ramey's store were several cars jacked up for tire changes. In broad daylight.

"Mr. Ramey," said the mayor, "you've got to cut that out."

At least that's what the mayor said he said to Mr. Ramey. Mr. Ramey says the mayor also said, "I'm going to put your bleep out of business"—not because of the cars jacked up on the street, but because of Mr. Ramey's involvement with plans to erect a police protest sign in the city.

The mayor denies all that. "He was breaking the law," the mayor stated, "and if my own father was violating the law, and I was in charge of enforcing it, I would enforce the law."

I heard Matt Dillon say that very same thing once to Miss Kitty over a few beers at the Long Branch.

I happen to think Mayor Jackson is absolutely correct in putting his foot down to stop the heinous practice of illegal car-jacking.

"It's a negative reflection on the city," he said. "There are oil spots on the street where he (Mr. Ramey) had cars out there changing tires."

Oil spots today, leaking transmission fluid puddles tomorrow, and pretty soon, the entire city is down the drain.

Just to prove he wasn't picking on J. K. Ramey, the mayor also pointed out another "bust" he made recently against another rampant crime spree in the city. Illegally parked cars.

The mayor was patroling in his trusty limo on Peachtree Street and spotted illegally parked cars in front of Salvatore's Restaurant.

"You better cut that out," he said to the owner of Salvatore's Restaurant. A couple of months later, the mayor made a routine check of Salvatore's again and, sure enough, he found two illegally parked cars in front of the restaurant. He called a wrecker and had them towed away.

Justice is swift at the hand of "Frontier Mayor" Maynard.

101

The mayor has also announced he is personally involved in trying to halt the rise of a couple of other crimes in our city.

Not murder. Not robbery. Not rape. But illegal newspapers on the street, and throwing things out of car windows.

"I see a newspaper on the street," the mayor said, "and I pick it up.

"I see somebody throw something out a car window," he continued, "and I stop them and make them come back and pick it up."

Does this man's bravery know no bounds?

Those same ungrateful people who complain about the mayor riding around town in his limo are probably saying now, if he's so effective at stopping crimes like jacking up cars and throwing garbage out of windows, why doesn't he also tackle such crimes as murder, robbery, and rape?

That's simple. "Frontier Mayor" Maynard is no dummy. Drive around in that big limo on the dark Atlanta streets where people are being murdered and robbed and raped in record numbers and he could get HIS bleep put out of business, too.

Permanently.

Pink Flamingos for MARTA

Atlanta's new rapid rail transit system successfully opened in July of 1979—just a few months after this column was written—WITHOUT expensive pieces of sculpture in the stations. You can't win 'em all, however. The inside of the Decatur station looks like the inside of the Holiday Inn Disco and Lounge at the airport in Oklahoma City.

Contrary to what you may have been led to believe, not everybody who has something to do with MARTA, Atlanta's public transportation company, is a dumbhead.

You take K. A. McMillon from suburban Gwinnett County. He is a member of the MARTA Development Committee. At a meeting of his committee this week, he actually stood up and said something that made good sense.

He said it was stupid to spend $145,000 on a sculpture MARTA was going to buy for one of its new rail stations.

"I think it's ridiculous we can't come to a meeting without having to listen to this garbage from the liberals who want to throw away MARTA's money," said Mr. McMillon.

He added, "I don't think we should spend any more on such as that until we've built the railroad first."

Two liberals fainted and another had to go to the bathroom when Mr. McMillon said that.

He is also against paying MARTA secretaries who don't know

their ampersands from a hole in the ground at Forsyth Street $20,000 a year, but he's saving that one for later.

The sculpture issue has been around for a while. Atlanta artist Curtis Patterson designed the piece for the new Hightower Station.

I was very interested to find out what a $145,000 piece of sculpture looks like. Thursday, I called around.

"Abstract steel," was one description.

"One of them modernistic-looking things," was another.

A MARTA official who swore he would break my neck if I quoted him said it was "a hunk of iron."

I eventually had to go straight to the artist himself. Strangely, Curtis Patterson wasn't talking.

"I am afraid anything I say will be misinterpreted," he said.

"You won't even describe your work to me?" I pressed on.

"No comment," he persisted.

The best I can determine, then, is that MARTA's $145,000 hunk of iron is abstract, modernistic, and is probably bigger than a bread box.

Mr. McMillon won out in his battle against the sculpture and the garbage-headed liberals. He persuaded four other members of the committee to vote with him against three who voted to purchase the sculpture. Hooray!

Supporters of the sculpture were very angry, because they said some type of art work was needed in MARTA rail stations to make them aesthetically pleasing to transit riders.

I agree. All K. A. McMillon and I are saying is, you can dress up a rail station and not have to fork over $145,000 for one piece of bent iron.

Those pink flamingos with the long legs they sell on the side of the highway are cheap, for instance. Throw a couple of those around the lot, and if there are any trees, you could always paint the trunks white.

And here's an idea: what happens to worn MARTA bus tires? What you can do with worn tires is move them over to the rail station, paint them white, and plant flowers inside them.

Hang a bullfighter picture or two, and you've got yourself one finely appointed rail station.

Also, you can usually count on the transit riders to do some decorating themselves. In New York, for instance, they paint colorful slogans like "Mao Lives!" and "Keel the Gringos" on station walls.

I would be willing to pop for maybe one big statue at the main MARTA station, a statue saluting all the people who paid the taxes that enabled MARTA to be constructed and provided jobs for a lot of fat cats.

Just show some poor sucker standing on a street corner with his pockets turned out and his collar turned up. And make him look hungry.

That modernistic enough for you?

5

Hail to the Chief!

The
Perfect
President

*I think it was my boyhood friend and idol, Weyman
C. Wannamaker, Jr., a great American, who said it
best. In the fifth grade, the teacher asked him,
"Weyman, would you like to be president when you
grow up?"*

*Weyman replied, "Hell, no. Only an idiot would
want to be president."*

being president used to be a nice job. Make a few
speeches, sign a few bills into law, declare war to rousing cheers,
go throw out the first ball at a Senators' game.

Practically everybody liked you, or at least respected the fact
you were doing the best you could. They played "Hail to the
Chief" and old men saluted and pretty girls smiled when your
train pulled into town.

But all that has changed. Being president now is like being
sentenced to four years of wearing your jockey shorts too
tight.

The president can't please anybody anymore. Our nation is
so diverse in its special interests and its needs and desires, that

the president automatically becomes the national whipping boy for everybody with a gripe.

Take Jimmy Carter. We elected him president because he wasn't a member of the Washington establishment. He was one of us, a simple peanut farmer from Georgia.

Read his reviews lately? Richard Nixon was in better shape, and he barely escaped a lynching on the White House lawn.

It seems a cinch now Jimmy Carter won't be reelected president in 1980. Why? Because he isn't a member of the Washington establishment, and what does a simple peanut farmer from Georgia know about being president?

Frankly, I don't think the Democrats can elect anybody president in 1980—not even Teddy Kennedy, who has terrific hair. Polls show Americans deserting the Democratic party in droves.

And who are the Republican choices? Howard Baker? Too slick. Robert Dole? Too slimy. John Connally? Too tricky. Ronald Reagan? Too dangerous. He's from California.

Name any potential candidate, and he has warts. Name any potential candidate, and I will name a faction that will eventually want his head on a platter.

Who we need for president is somebody who is perfect.

I've got just the guy.

We need a president who can unite us again, someone who can bring Anita Bryant together with the Gay Liberationists. Bring Joan Baez together with Jane Fonda. Bring Martin and Lewis together again for *Jumping Jacks II*.

We need a president who can get this country moving, who can give us an energy program that will fill the tank of every big, black Buick from Maine to California at thirty cents a gallon.

If anybody could pull off that miracle, you say, why not get him to raise the dead, too? Stay tuned.

Could he help the farmers? Of course he could. He could lower the price of fertilizer and raise the price of peas so fast the farmers would be dancing in their fields rather than clogging up the interstate with tractorcades.

Same for the truckers. Could he help the truckers in their fight against high diesel-fuel prices and idiotic government regulations? Does a semi hauling hogs pollute?

Taxes. Now there is a problem. The people with the least money pay the most taxes. My candidate would jump on that imbalance feet first.

He knows what it means to be poor. If you think Abe Lincoln had it tough as a kid, you should have seen where this guy was born.

Human rights? My man with the plan for 1980 swears by human rights. No, he doesn't. He doesn't swear. Or drink, or smoke, or lust.

SALT II? Who needs it? The Russians would be eating out of his hands.

Feed the starving? He could do it. It's a long story, but nobody knows more about how to make a little food go a long way.

My candidate could bridge all our gaps, solve all our problems. He could make George Meany a sweetie.

And if elected, there would be no need to change the towels in the White House. He has the same initials as the current president.

Unfortunately, he's probably too busy to run. But the poor sucker who winds up with the job in 1980 will still be expected to live up to all his standards.

It's the new fact of life for the American presidency. If you can't walk on water, you need not apply.

First Sister

You must admit, the Carter family has been one of the most colorful in the nation's history of presidential families. "Colorful" is a nice way to say it.

my first thought when I read about the president's sister Gloria being arrested for playing a harmonica in a late-night diner in Americus was, so let her play it.

That is mild compared to other things I have seen people do in late-night diners. I have seen egg-throwings, plate-breakings, cigarette-machine destroyings, domestic-quarrelings, and one night I saw a man dump his grits on the floor because they were lumpy.

And they most certainly were. When he dumped them on the floor, they didn't splatter. They rolled underneath the jukebox, causing an electrical shortage right in the middle of Conway Twitty and Loretta Lynn's duet.

The president's sister, Gloria Spann—heretofore known mostly for riding on motorcycles and in tractorcades—told her version of the incident in Tuesday's papers.

She and her husband and some friends went to the McWaffles restaurant in Americus early Sunday morning for a late snack. Gloria broke into "I'm so Lonesome I Could Cry" on her harmonica. She would have been happy to play something else, but that's the only tune she knows.

Moments later, a waitress came to her table and asked that she cut out the harmonica. The other customers were complaining they couldn't hear the jukebox.

No way. "Back me into a corner," says Gloria, "and I'll come out blowing my harmonica." That's the old Carter family spirit. Too bad Jimmy can't use it. As many corners as he's been in lately, he'd need a symphony orchestra with extra tubas to get out.

The waitress was no pushover, either. She called the law. It's not every night you get a call to a diner where the sister of the president of the United States is playing her harmonica so the other customers can't hear the jukebox.

But Americus was ready. Three police cars showed up to quell the disturbance. Gloria and her husband were arrested for refusing to leave the restaurant when three carloads of policemen asked them to.

"Good thing I didn't bring my guitar," Gloria said. "I might have gotten five years."

There are two sides to every story, of course. I called the restaurant to get the other side. The manager came to the phone. Her name is Chrystal Bailey. She said there was trouble with harmonicat Gloria and her gang the minute they walked in.

"We have a rule on the weekend you have to order from the counter after eleven o'clock," Chrystal said. "That's because we get so many in here who are wild and drinkin'. I couldn't keep help because they didn't want to go to the tables and serve people like that.

"This group wouldn't order from the counter. They wanted table service. I didn't know who she (Gloria) was, but it wouldn't have mattered. If I gave her table service, I'd have to give it to everybody else, too, and then I wouldn't have anybody still working here.

"They got loud, and they got rowdy. I'm not against anybody having a good time, but they were disturbing others, and they were asked twice to be quiet.

"I can't have that. This place used to be really bad when it was a Hasty House because of such carrying-on. We've tried to get rid of that reputation."

I asked Chrystal Bailey if she thought the Spann party might possibly have been drinking before their arrival at McWaffles.

"I do," she said. "I think drinkin' is what it was."

I can't blame Gloria and her friends for that. Not everybody who goes into a late-night diner has been out boozing; but it helps. Sober, you would notice the grease hanging in the air and the tattoos on the cook's arms, and that might spoil your appetite.

Now that I have finally reached the bottom of all this, I think the entire matter has been blown out of proportion. Playing harmonica in a late-night diner is no big deal, but Chrystal Bailey has her problems, too.

So what's the big fuss about? A day without one of the president's relatives getting into hot water and embarrassing the White House would be like a day without new allegations against Bert Lance.

What we should do is be thankful there was another Carter to take up the slack until Billy gets out of the hospital.

The Plain(s)
Truth About
Killer Rabbits

I'll bet covering Millard Fillmore was never this much fun . . .

it's not that I didn't believe President Carter when he reported being attacked by a "killer rabbit" during his recent fishing trip in Plains, but my vast knowledge of rabbits has left me with a number of questions I would like to ask him about the "attack."

I know a lot about rabbits, because I spent a great portion of my boyhood trying to trap one in a box. The idea is, prop a box on a stick and put something under the box a rabbit might like to eat.

When the rabbit goes under the box to take the bait, he knocks away the stick and the box falls down over him, and you have yourself a rabbit.

Sounds good on paper, but it doesn't work. The rabbit will take the bait every time, but he is also smart enough to avoid contact with the stick, and I wasted a lot of good lettuce and carrots and okra—rabbits like okra, believe it or not—before I realized that fact.

What else I know about rabbits is (a) they are lousy swimmers, (b) they are afraid of their own shadows, and (c) the president has been under a great deal of stress and strain lately, which had nothing to do with rabbits until one tried to attack his canoe in the middle of a South Georgia pond.

Since the White House would not even release an alleged

photograph of the rabbit in question—some clever soul called it a "Banzai Bunny"—I don't suppose I will ever get the opportunity to question the president face-to-face on the matter.

I won't, however, be pushed aside that easily. When the man with his finger on the nuclear button starts seeing killer rabbits in ponds, I think it is time the American people got an explanation.

I submit the following list of questions to the president as a public service. Dare he not respond?

1. Have you, Mr. President, ever had similar experiences?

2. If so, how often?

3. Are these experiences often accompanied by headaches and/or dizzy spells?

4. Was Hamilton Jordan along on the trip?

5. Did he see the rabbit, too?

6. Your report concerning the incident said the rabbit, as it attacked your canoe, was "hissing menacingly." Did at any time the rabbit make a sound that could be called a "snort"?

7. Did Hamilton Jordan at any time make such a sound?

8. How tall was the rabbit?

9. One foot? Two feet?

10. Think deeply, Mr. President, but could the rabbit have been as tall as SIX feet?

11. When you were a little boy in Plains, Mr. President, did you have, uh, "playmates" that were not really there?

12. Were any of them rabbits?

13. Did you talk to them and play fun games with them, and when Miss Lillian prepared your lunch, did you ask her to set an extra place for them?

14. How old were you when Miss Lillian explained to you that people were beginning to talk about your, uh, "playmates"?

15. As a child, were you ever completely shut out at an

116

Easter egg hunt and the other children threw rocks at you and called you names because your basket was empty?

16. If I say, "Here comes Peter Cottontail, hopping down the bunny trail, hippity-hoppity, Easter's on its way," what is the first thing that comes into your mind?

17. The report of the incident said you "beat back" the rabbit with your canoe paddle. As a childish prank, Mr. President, did you ever put your cat in a dryer at the laundromat?

18. Are you absolutely certain the animal that attacked your canoe was a rabbit?

19. Could it have been a beaver? An otter with long ears?

20. Bob Dole in his bunny pajamas?

Who's Ready for Teddy?

It should become very obvious while reading this that I do not consider Teddy Kennedy to be one of the great leaders of our time. I do think he looks nice in a suit, however.

there was one big headline after another recently concerning Ted Kennedy's entry into the 1980 presidential race. Some of the news was earthshaking.

- First, Teddy's mom said it was OK for him to run.
- Second, Teddy's wife said if he got elected she would go live with him in the White House. I thought that was big of her.
- Third, Teddy allegedly thinks of President Carter as a "political cripple" and told Carter he'd be smart to go beat a rabbit in the head and leave the presidenting to him.
- Fourth, everybody involved said that was a bunch of "horse manure."
- Fifth, President Carter's mom, Miss Lillian, got into the act, too. She said if Teddy runs she hopes "nothing happens to him."

According to news reports, Miss Lillian's statement, made at a chicken barbecue in New Hampshire, sent a shock wave through the Democratic party.

Jerry Brown was there. He was shocked. State Democratic party chairman Romeo Dorval was there. He was shocked, too. So were Kennedy backers in the audience.

118

They were so shocked, they booed Miss Lillian (who is eighty-one). I wasn't shocked. I happen to think if you are eighty-one, you can say anything you damn well please, especially if your son is the president and you've been on "The Johnny Carson Show" a couple of times.

There has always been something about Teddy Kennedy that bothered me, but I could never quite put my finger on it.

Now I know what it is. It is not Teddy who bothers me so much; it is people who think he would make a good president.

They really don't know why Teddy Kennedy would make a good president, and they boo little old eighty-one-year-old ladies.

"Why do you think he would make a good president?" I have asked a number of draft-Kennedyites recently.

"Because," begins the usual reply, "he, uh, well . . .

"he, uh, LOOKS like a president."

I have heard that, uh, brilliant line of political thinking before. That's how Henry Fonda got his part in *Fail Safe*, but, unfortunately, we aren't casting a movie here.

So what do you LOOK like when you look like a president?

I remember a calendar we had in elementary school. It had the pictures of all the presidents, up through Eisenhower, who had just been elected president.

Ike was bald and looked like he had just knocked his tee shot in the lake at the par-three twelfth at Augusta National.

Herbert Hoover looked uncomfortable, Abe Lincoln had a big nose, and although you couldn't tell it by his picture on the calendar, George Washington had bad teeth.

Teddy Kennedy has long hair, a pleasant smile, and he wears dopey glasses to make himself look more sophisticated. They said the same thing about Warren G. Harding.

119

I did find one Kennedy backer willing to list some other qualifications Teddy has to be president. Relax, this will only take a second:

- He has a good speaking voice.
- His mother is a courageous person.
- He probably learned a lot about running the country from his two brothers.

Brilliant. I was sitting here trying to think of a way to end this, and I just thought of it. What do you say to people when they fumble and stumble and try to tell you why they think Teddy Kennedy, just another pretty face who got a big break the day he was born, would make a good president?

You say, uh, two little words.

Horse manure.

The Official
Candidate
Quiz

I wrote this one cold afternoon during the 1980
New Hampshire primary. I seriously doubt I
was sober at the time.

n Manchester, N. H.
ow that we have completed caucuses in Iowa and
Maine and primaries here in New Hampshire, with extensive
news coverage of all three, it is high time the voters of America
were well acquainted with the candidates who want to be their
next president.

This is the beauty of a system that no longer allows its
presidential nominees to be hand-picked in smoke-filled rooms.
The people finally have something to do with the nomination
process.

You may be asking yourself, "I think I am up-to-date on the
candidates and the issues, but how can I be certain?"

Worry not. To get a reading on your knowledge of the 1980
presidential race, all you need do is take the following test which
asks pertinent questions concerning the run for the White House.

The test, concocted by yours truly, who has been trapped in
New Hampshire with babbling brooks and babbling political-
types for what seems like months, is simple and easy to
understand.

Mark your answers with a No. 2 lead pencil only, and make
no unnecessary smudges or marks on the test paper. Correct
answers will be printed in the classified ad section of the Fargo,
North Dakota, *Fleaflicker-Herald* on Inauguration Day, 1981.

121

If you answer all the questions correctly, you are qualified to read a Joseph Kraft political column and then pretend you understood it. If you miss less than five, you probably remember who Tom Eagleton was. If you miss between five and ten, you probably think Dewey hung on to win, and if you miss more than that, your penalty should be a week locked in a room with a Right-to-Lifer, an opponent of gun control, Paul Harvey, and two anti-nukes who are protesting the Three-Mile Island incident by refusing to bathe.

The test follows. Take as long as necessary to complete. Ready? Begin.

1. Of the following, pick the most boring aspect of President Jimmy Carter's current administration.

A. His hemorrhoid condition. B. Walter Mondale.

2. Which of the previously held positions would Republican candidate George Bush say helped him LEAST in preparing him for the possibility of serving as president?

A. Congressman from Texas. B. Head of the CIA. C. Ambassador to China. D. Houston Roto-Rooter man.

3. Ronald Reagan was born in:

A. 1612. B. 1613. C. 1614. D. 1615. E. Poland.

4. The primary difference between Reagan and fellow Republican candidate John Anderson is:

A. Grecian Formula 9.

5. Which of the following are LEAST likely to win the 1980 Democratic nomination?

A. Hodding Carter. B. Bo Derek C. The Fog. D. Jerry Brown.

6. True or false: Republican Philip Crane of Illinois is a figment of his imagination.

7. Who is shorter than a fire hydrant and speaks with a Southern Accent?

A. Little Jimmy Dickens. B. Amy Carter. C. A Vidalia onion. D. Howard Baker.

8. In the space provided below, list all the intelligent comments rock singer Linda Ronstadt made while campaigning in New Hampshire for boyfriend Jerry Brown.

9. Robert Dole is:

A. A senator from Kansas. B. A former vice-presidential candidate. C. A pineapple. D. Wasting his time. E. All of the above.

10. Which of the following embarrassing situations DID NOT involve Ted Kennedy?

A. Chappaquiddick. B. CBS interview with Roger Mudd. C. Harvard cheating scandal. D. Idiotic comments concerning the Shah of Iran. E. Seward's Folly.

11. President Carter has called for an American boycott of the 1980 Summer Olympics in Moscow. Challenger Kennedy's alternatives to that are:

A. Boycotting the 1980 NBA playoffs, instead.

12. One of the lesser-known candidates who ran in the New Hampshire Democratic primary is named "LaRouche." His first name is:

A. Anita. B. Boom-Boom. C. Lady Bird. D. Lash.

13. Former President Gerald Ford would like to throw his hat into the 1980 political ring, but he can't remember where he put his hat. Where would you suggest he look?

A. In his closet. B. In his golf bag. C. Under his pillow. D. On his head.

14. True or false? John Connally.

Political Pain
in the
"Neck"

Another problem with being president is
somebody is always sticking his nose in your,
uh, business.

things have been tough for the president lately. Egypt
and Israel still can't come to terms for peace, there has been no
SALT agreement, angry farmers disrupted his holiday visit to
Plains, and then there was the messy business of kicking Taiwan
out of bed in favor of Red China.

I have a great deal of faith in the president, however, and I
am certain he will eventually find a way to deal with those
lingering issues.

But one other problem facing President Carter could lead to
his eventual downfall. It might even become the battleground on
which the Republicans decide to fight for reentry into the White
House in 1980.

The president of the United States, the honorable James
Earl Carter, Jr., has a bad case of hemorrhoids.

I am all for the public's right to know, but I was a bit shocked
when the news of the president's condition came blasting over the
radio one evening during the holidays.

How did such private information leak out? I called one of
my White House sources to find out.

"We tried our best to keep it quiet," he said, "but the

president sent Jody Powell out for 'Preparation H' and that was the ballgame."

"Preparation H" is the medicine most prescribed by doctors for relief of the painful condition known as hemorrhoids.

When I first heard the news, I laughed. But then I realized the painful condition known as hemorrhoids is no laughing matter, especially when it is the president of a large, powerful nation who has them.

"He's hurting and he's hurting bad," *Newsweek* magazine quoted a White House spokesperson as saying about President Carter's case.

It is probably not in good taste to discuss exactly what hemorrhoids are and how they affect their victims. But they make it hurt where you sit and often cause drastic changes in the sufferer's personality.

I once worked for a man who had hemorrhoids. Most of the time, he was the nicest guy you would ever want to meet. When his condition flared up, he was Attila the Hun with a hangover.

During a particularly painful bout with his ailment, he attempted suicide in the middle of the office as a means of relief. Only the actions of a quick-thinking secretary saved his life.

Two weeks later, when the pain returned, he fired her. A man suffering from hemorrhoids cannot be held responsible for his actions.

Which brings me back to the president. Suppose he had another flareup in the middle of serious negotiations with, say, Soviet President Brezhnev?

The pain having siphoned his good senses, who knows what the president might say in the midst of a testy situation?

"Leonid, you pork-faced imbecile!" is simply not good diplomatic phraseology.

I can hear the Republicans asking the question of the American people already: Can we feel secure knowing the leader of the free world, the man with his finger on the nuclear button, is suffering from the horrid fate and agony of you-know-what?

"It's a ticklish situation for sure," admitted my White House source.

"Ticklish?" I asked.

"Poor choice of words," he replied. "But I think the president can handle it. He's had experience with this sort of thing all his life, you know."

I didn't know. The president has had hemorrhoids all his life?

My source explained. "First, he had to grow up with a brother like Billy. Then, when he was governor, he had to deal with Lester Maddox.

"Now, he's got the farmers on him, the Taiwanese are marching, the Iranian dissidents are mad because he has supported the Shah, Ted Kennedy may run against him in '80, and Barry Goldwater has called him a coward."

But what, I asked, do they have to do with hemorrhoids?

"They're all a big pain in the . . . "

"Neck?" I interrupted.

"Have it your way." said my source.

6

It's Been One Hassle After Another

Looking
for
Mr. Goodwrench

How many days does it take me to screw in a light bulb? Four. Three to fool around with it myself, and one to round up an electrician to finish the job.

a man from the city water department came to my house last week and cut off my water. He had some absurd reason for doing that. I think he mentioned I hadn't paid my bill on time.

I attempted to explain. Maybe there were some goats in the neighborhood, and one was nosing around in my mailbox and ate my payment to the city water department.

You can't explain *anything* to a man with a wrench.

So there I was for a couple of days, with no water. It was a learning experience.

I learned it is virtually impossible to brush your teeth using orange juice.

I learned if you wet your face with milk and then try to shave, the pain will be incredible.

I learned if you don't shower for a couple of days, you won't have to put up with worrisome people like your friends and fellow employees.

129

I learned if you don't wash coffee cups, something green will grow inside of them.

I also learned that I still don't know anything about anything that is mechanical in nature. I couldn't change the oil in my salad.

Here's what happened:

I finally reached the city water department—the telephone there had been busy for forty-eight hours—and the woman who answered agreed with me that it was probably all a big mistake that my water had been cut off.

She apologized on behalf of the mayor and the city for the inconvenience and said if I would pay my bill, along with an additional six-dollar service charge, the man with the wrench would return to my house and turn the water back on.

Naturally, I accepted her apology and her kind offer to right the department's wrong.

I returned home that evening, expecting to find running water. Instead, I found a note in my door from Mr. Goodwrench.

"Dear Sir," it began, "I turned the water back on in your meter. However, I left it off in your property valve because of an indication there was a faucet open in your house.

"You can turn the water on in your property valve. It is located approximately twelve inches down in a metal pipe that is located approximately ten feet behind your water meter. Thanks."

Thank you. But I don't know anything about water meters and property valves. I can barely operate my shower curtain.

I called the water department again, and they tried to explain to me where to locate my property valve. They tried to explain it several times.

"You'd better talk to Mr. Something-or-Other," a woman said. Mr. Something-or-Other became impatient and said, "If you don't know where your property valve is, you'll just have to look in your yard until you find it."

130

It was raining outside. I searched for my property valve for half an hour. It occurred to me that I wouldn't know my property valve if it walked up to me and played the flute.

I called the department again. It was after five o'clock Friday afternoon. I went into Plan "B." I started crying.

Another half-hour search, and I finally located what I determined to be my water meter. It was located in some tall grass I should cut, but when I pull the starter cord on my lawn mower, nothing happens.

I walked approximately ten feet behind my water meter and, sure enough, there was a metal pipe like the note said. I reached twelve inches inside it and, sure enough, there was my property valve, along with a lot of dirt and bugs and worms.

I suffered a mild coronary, ruined a shirt and a pair of pants, but I finally turned my property valve and immediately felt a sensation of great satisfaction.

I went back inside my house, took a shower, and watered the green things growing in the coffee cups.

I Hate
the
Beach

*I forgot to mention one other thing that will
drive a person crazy at the beach. Is there a
more uncomfortable feeling on this earth than
pulling on a cold, wet bathing suit?*

eKiawah Island, S. C.
very six months or so I get a little crazy in the city and I
say to myself, "What I need are a few days at the beach."

So here I am at Kiawah Island, near Charleston. Kiawah
Island used to be inhabited by bugs, large birds, and alligators,
but then some smart money from Kuwait came in and built
condominiums, a golf course, tennis courts, and one of those
trinket shops where a lamp made out of sea shells costs $175.

I like my room here at the Kiawah Inn. It overlooks the
shimmering Atlantic, and at these prices, I will turn the
thermostat down to any level I please.

Scenes from the nearby low-country marsh adorn the walls,
and the soap in the bathroom is individually boxed.

At Howard Johnsons and Holiday Inns, the soap in the
bathroom comes wrapped in paper. How gauche.

What I don't like about Kiawah Island, and what I don't like
about all seaside resorts, is the beach itself. I never thought I
would admit this, but I have been a closet beach-hater for years.

What I hate most about the beach is the sand. If beaches had
outdoor carpet or Astro-Turf, maybe I would feel differently.
Sand is the pits.

132

There is no way to go to the beach without getting completely covered with sand. Sand in your topsiders, sand in your hair, sand in your bologna sandwiches, and if you are not careful, sand in your bathing trunks.

Sand in your bathing trunks makes a person crabby and uncomfortable and causes all sorts of unspeakable rashes.

Once you are covered with sand, it is impossible to wash it all off. No matter how long you shower after a day at the beach, there will always be sand in your bed.

Cracker crumbs in your bed are just as bad as sand in your bed, but I would rather sleep with a South Carolina three-eyed marsh hog than with sand or cracker crumbs.

I also hate the sun at the beach. Two minutes in the sun, and I look like I've been roasted on the devil's own spit. People with nothing better to do but lie around getting suntans DESERVE skin cancer and early wrinkling and smelling like *eau de Valvoline*.

Another thing I dislike about the beach is young, musclebound boys with deep tans who cavort in skimpy bathing suits and throw frisbees. Throwing frisbees is a mindless exercise designed for people with the IQs of jellyfish, which is another reason the beach is no place for the sane.

What's under that water? Jellyfish, stingrays, things with no eyes, things with teeth, like sharks. Once I read what to do in case you are in the water and a shark approaches.

"Do not run. Do not splash water. Do not shout. Wait until the shark swims close enough and then strike it on the head with a blunt instrument."

Fine. I'll just stand here without running or splashing water or shouting, and when the shark swims close enough, I'll pull this tire tool I keep in the pocket of my bathing trunks and belt him right between his bloodthirsty eyes.

I could go on. I could even make a tacky remark like, may a giant oil spill cover every beach in the world and see if I care.

But I won't. A lot of people enjoy the beach. Children, muscle-brains, and exhibitionists, for instance.

Let them all go bake their brains. I'll just sit here in my room in my overcoat and play with the knobs on my air conditioner.

Return of the Wethead

If every man in America would stop using his electric hair dryer for one week, we could save enough in energy costs to send a dozen kids to barber school. Think about it.

i took a long look at my electric hair dryer the other morning. It was a Christmas gift, and I cherished it once. Its sleek, modern styling hinted macho, but at the same time said its owner would be a man of sensitivity, a man in touch with the necessity for good grooming habits.

I recall how the handle felt in my hand the morning of that first dry. It fit perfectly. It was a part of me, an added appendage for countless mornings to come.

I began in warm, shifted to medium in mid-dry, and then gunned it to high for the finish. My hair fluffed as it had never fluffed before. One spark, however, and meet the human torch.

I realize there are a number of important issues that probably should be discussed in a forum such as this, but occasionally, the real issues of the day are hidden deep behind the headlines. Occasionally, one must stand and be heard on a matter that at first glance might seem trivial.

The time has come, America, to speak out on the electric hair dryer for men.

It came to me as I stood, nurd-like, holding my dryer to my head. Like all mornings, I had showered and shampooed with a

135

shampoo the fragrance of blossoming apricots, the color of the dawning sky.

This, I thought , is ridiculous. This is insane. This is a horrid, useless waste of time I can do without.

I figure I have spent five minutes every morning for the past five years blow-drying my hair. That is six days of my life spent with Flash Gordon's ray gun pointed at my brain, which probably has windburn by now.

It all began with cosmetics commercials screaming at us on television. Our forefathers rallied behind "54-40 or Fight!" and "Remember the Alamo!" and "A Chicken in Every Pot!" For this generation, it has been, "The Wethead Is Dead!" Pour out your Wildroot Creme Oil, Charlie, it's a blow-dry kind of day.

What followed was a mad rush by America's male population to grow hair. Then dry it. Then spray it so it wouldn't budge in a hurricane. No longer did men comb their hair. They raked it. Hair wasn't "cut," it was "styled."

Ears disappeared from Maine to California, and ten million bottles of Vitalis sat lonely and gathering dust, an oily relic of the past.

Young and old alike, we all bought electric hair dryers. Even athletes and probably truck drivers.

I know not what course others may take, but as for me, I have plugged in my electric hair dryer for the last time.

I despise the effort and time wasted on it, and I despise its high-pitched hum. Put an electric hair dryer to your head and you couldn't hear the 7:05 flight to Cleveland take off in the kitchen.

Left completely alone, I have discovered, hair will dry itself in less than an hour. I will save time, conserve energy, and never be mistaken for a skinny sheepdog again.

I threw my electric hair dryer in the garbage. Along with my banana creme rinse somebody said would give my hair body. I don't want body. Along with my shampoo the fragrance of

136

blossoming apricots. The fragrance of blossoming apricots is for girls and boys who drink whiskey sours and eat the cherries.

Join me if you dare, men. Wetheads, arise again and stand tall! If you must, even slick it down and part it on the side and look up your old barber.

You never know. He may still be in business.

The Doctor, Revisited

*My doctor read this and called me in for an
immediate reexamination. I was sore for a
month.*

it had been a long time since my last complete physical
examination, and I was in no hurry to have another one.

When I was eleven, a doctor examined me from head to toe
before my trip to Camp Thunder and pronounced me fit for
everything from overnight hiking trips to towel fights in the
shower.

I didn't want to go to Camp Thunder and secretly hoped he
would find some horrible malady like bumps on my head, which
would have kept me away from camp and couldn't have been as
bad as the towel fights in the showers there.

A towel fight in a shower involves inflicting physical harm
upon a fellow camper. My boyhood friend and idol, Weyman C.
Wannamaker, Jr., a great American, was the king of the towel
fighters.

He would wet one end of a large beach towel and fling that
lethal end toward the uncovered hindparts of his victim, snapping
it back on impact with a resounding, "Whap!"

Bend over to retrieve your soap in a shower with Weyman C.
Wannamaker, Jr., and his beach towel, and you would be
standing for campfire vespers the entire week.

I had no bumps on my head when I was eleven, and I went on

138

to Camp Thunder. I solved the towel fight problem. I didn't take a shower for seven days.

I sat alone at campfire vespers. But I sat.

I don't know what came over me last week to have another physical examination. Doctors spook me. Their offices spook me. Their nurses spook me, and all their receptionists just got off the boat from Transylvania where their last jobs were in a blood bank.

"You vil take a seat, please," they begin. "It vil only be a little while."

It vil never be a little while. It vil be an eternity if you are as frightened of doctors as I am. Doctors' offices even smell like impending doom.

Last week, while I waited for my doctor, I tried to read a magazine. Why are magazines in doctors' offices always out of date?

I picked up a *Newsweek*. Roosevelt was on the cover. Teddy.

My doctor was a nice enough fellow. First, he asked me a lot of questions.

Do you smoke?

Yes.

Do you drink?

Yes.

Do you eat regular, balanced meals?

No.

Do you get plenty of rest and exercise?

No.

Do you even get dizzy spells?

Only when I run out of cigarettes or have a drink before "The Today Show" goes off the air.

Then, he took me into a small room with only one door, which he closed, and examined me. He examined my head, my nose, my ears, my throat, my neck, my chest, my back, my stomach, my legs, my feet, and my toes.

I still don't have any bumps on my head, but one of my toes has an ingrown nail which he mashed, prompting a scream. That is how he pays his receptionist. She loves screaming.

He did other things to my person as well, but I can't mention any of them here except to say they were indignities that shouldn't happen to a rabid dog.

"It's for your own good," the doctor said.

Jack the Ripper told his patients the same thing.

Later, he turned me over to a nurse who put needles in me and gave me an X-ray. I have also wondered why, if there is nothing dangerous about X-rays, the nurse who administers them always stands behind a lead screen?

The doctor didn't put it in so many words, but I suppose I will live.

Otherwise, the receptionist—Countess Rubellina in the old country—wouldn't have asked, "Vil you be paying now, or shall ve bill you later?"

"Later, sweetheart," I said. "Later."

Deliver Me
From
Sausage Balls

I even know people who give cocktail parties
you go to before you go to another cocktail
party. Isn't being grown-up fun?

Standing around at a cocktail party the other evening, in honor of somebody getting married or getting a divorce or running for president—I forget which—the thought suddenly occurred to me, "I'm sick of standing around at cocktail parties."

I don't have an actual count, but I am certain I have been to somewhere near a million cocktail parties since I became old enough to stop cruising around in a car drinking beer, which is what you do until you become old enough to get invited to cocktail parties.

At first, I thought cocktail parties were sort of neat. The booze was free, and normally in great abundance, and before I had eaten several thousands of those little sausage balls they always serve as an *hors d'oeuvre*, I thought they were quite tasty. Now, the very mention of one makes me quite ill.

And, after a time, I found myself actually dreading cocktail parties and concocting all sorts of excuses to get out of them.

My best excuse to get out of a cocktail party is, "Thank you very much for inviting me, but I'm supposed to be involved in a serious automobile accident that evening."

Americans will give a cocktail party for nearly every occasion and for nearly everybody.

I have been to cocktail parties in honor of Canadian consuls,

Japanese piano players, a man from Louisiana who makes duck calls, the birth of twins, the buying of a new house, the selling of an old one, the opening of a play, and the closing of a number of newspapers and magazines and even a used-car dealership. (The owner had liquidated with plans to go into the ministry. It's a long story.)

Regardless of the occasion, however, all cocktail parties are generally alike.

● There is never anywhere to sit down, and it is my firm belief that drinking is a sit-down sort of endeavor.

● You get drunker faster when you drink standing up and are therefore more liable to do something you will regret the next day.

● Somebody always does something he regrets the next day, like saying *Kramer vs. Kramer* stunk, or barging in on the hostess in the bathroom.

● You have to talk a lot at a cocktail party, and the conversation is always the same. Dull, unless someone knows some juicy gossip about somebody who wasn't invited.

● You can never find an ashtray.

● While you are listening to some juicy gossip and eating one of those little chicken wings, which are always near the sausage balls, the little plate where you are supposed to put your bones will be taken away, and you will have to stand there like an idiot holding one of those little chicken-wing bones.

● The solution to that problem is to find a person you don't like and drop the bone into his or her coat pocket while he or she isn't looking.

There simply must be more original ways for people to gather and bore one another.

Charades, for instance. Terrific game. You make a complete fool of yourself, just like at a cocktail party, but this way you have all the guests' undivided attention while you do it.

142

Croquet. Remember croquet? Everybody gathers in the back yard and knocks the little balls through the wire hoops. Nobody really likes to play croquet because it's a stupid game, but at least you don't have to talk.

I can think of all sorts of alternatives to cocktail parties. Doesn't anybody give wienie roasts anymore? What about hayrides?

Hayrides are for bumpkins, you say. Hayrides are kid stuff. That's all you know.

Once I went on a hayride with Kathy Sue Loudermilk, bless her heart. I was gone six days and woke up in Ocala, Florida, with a tattoo.

That, believe me, beats the absolute fool out of standing around half-crocked trying to talk to a Japanese piano player with a mouthful of sausage balls.

Interviewing
Miss
Fruit Fly

*I admit it. This is one of those columns I wrote
because I didn't have anything else to write
about. I still don't want to interview any little
girl ice skaters, however.*

a lot of people call and write suggesting ideas for
columns. I appreciate that. It should be obvious by now I need all
the help I can get.

But not all the ideas I get are good ones. In fact, some of the
ideas I get are insane.

There is a man who writes to suggest a column about him
because he is Jesus. You would be surprised how many people
think they are Jesus.

"I have followed your work closely," he says, "and I want you
to be the first to have my story."

It's a dilly, I admit, but I've already heard it.

Out of sheer curiosity, I called the man who thinks he is
Jesus. I got a recording. "This is Jesus Christ," it began. "I have
stepped away for a few moments . . . . "

Another group of people who want to be written about are
people who think they know who really killed John Kennedy. I
think there are more of them than people who think they are
Jesus.

"Can you talk?" a voice asked on the other end of the
telephone.

"About what?" I replied.

144

"About what happened in Dallas."

A sports nut, I figured.

"I know who really killed JFK," said the voice.

"Who?" I asked, off the top of my head.

"I'll have to call you back," the voice said. "I hear the nurse coming."

Another group of nuts who want publicity are nuts who own talking animals. Talking dogs, talking cats, talking mules, talking rabbits, talking pigs, and the woman who called to say she had taught her parakeet to recite the pledge of allegiance to the flag.

The parakeet's name was Cindy.

"Cindy's so smart," said the woman, "next, I'm going to teach her to sing 'God Bless America.' "

God bless a milk cow before I'm going to interview a flag-waving parakeet that thinks it's Kate Smith.

In order to save us all a lot of trouble, I have compiled a list of other things I refuse to write columns about. I don't want to offend anyone, but if you were planning to call or write to suggest any of the following, go talk to your cat and leave me alone:

● BALLOON RACES: I am not interested in balloon races. I am not interested in balloon racers. I get all the hot air I can handle interviewing politicians.

If you can figure out a way to get rid of politicians by floating them away in balloons, call me.

● LITTLE GIRL ICE SKATERS: I don't have anything against little girl ice skaters. I just don't want to talk to one. After you have asked a little girl ice skater, "Do you really enjoy ice skating?" and her mother has answered, "She just looooooves it," that's the ballgame.

Besides, all little girl ice skaters grow up to marry quarterbacks, which is what can happen if you spend too much time spinning your brain around.

145

● RATTLESNAKE HUNTS: Television stations love rattle-snake hunts because they can get film of some clod walking around with a sackful of live rattlesnakes and peddle it at eleven o'clock as news. I am interested in rattlesnake hunts only if somebody is bitten at one, preferably somebody from a television station.

I agree with philosopher Dupree Jenkins, who once pointed out, "Finding a rattlesnake when you are looking for one is not exciting. When you ain't, and you find one anyway, now there's an attention-grabber."

● BEAUTY QUEENS: Ever try to interview Miss Fruit Fly?

● MISTREATMENT OF BABY SEALS: If I knew any baby seals personally, I might feel differently. I'd rather help the rattlesnakes. People are all the time milking rattlesnakes, poking forked sticks in their faces and taking them to weirdo churches. You'd bite back, too.

● SOCCER: If we ignore soccer long enough, I am convinced it will finally go away.

● RUGBY: See "SOCCER."

● UFO SIGHTINGS: Don't tell me about UFOs, bring me one. Put it on my desk and let me talk to the driver. Otherwise, go sniff some more swamp gas.

● TROUBLES WITH THE IRS: About this time every year, I begin to hear from people complaining about how they've been screwed by the IRS. I don't want to hear your whining and petty gripes. It is the duty of every American citizen to pay his or her taxes cheerfully and respectfully.

Besides, I don't want to be reminded of what the lousy bloodsuckers are trying to do to me.

146

How I
Stop Pedxxx
Smookxing

To be quite honest, I did write the following piece without a cigarette, and I am proud to announce I finally kicked the nasty tobacco habit after fifteen years. Do I still want a cigarette occasionally? Given a chance, I would eat one.

i am going to attempt the impossible. I am going to attempt to write this entire column without smoking a cigarette. I have never written anything without relying heavily on the soul of tobacco.

The doctor was firm in his insistence I give up a fifteen-year, two-pack-a-day habit.

"And what if I don't?" I asked him.

"A number of things could happen," he answered. "All of them end in somebody collecting your life insurance a lot sooner than you expected."

I have tried to stop smoking before. A friend and I agreed to stop smoking together. We made it eight days. I called his home one evening to see how he was doing. His wife answered the phone.

"He smoked a cigarette," she said. "He was sitting in a chair watching television. Suddenly, he got out of the chair, jumped up on the coffee table, lit a cigarette, and looked to the sky and said, 'God wants me to smoke!' "

147

It made sense that if God wanted my friend to smoke, He would have felt the same about me.

There are a number of things I can do without having a cigarette while I am doing them. I don't need a cigarette while sleeping, swimming, taking a shower, playing with dynamite, or eating collards.

But write without a cigarette?

So far, I have made it this far, but I have begun to hallucinate, which always happens to me when I attempt to quit smoking. A penguin just walked into the office.

It would be just about here I would normally have a cigarette while writing a column. I need both hands to type, so I would stop typing, pull one out of the pack, light it, take two or three puffs and return to the typewriter.

Sometimes when I smoke while writing my column, I forget I am smoking and the cigarette burns down to a point where it falls out of the ashtray.

That is very dangerous with all the paper that is usually strewn about my desk. Last week, the April issue of *Playboy*, my desk calendar, and a press release from the annual Armadillo Confab and Exposition in Victoria, Texas, were burned to a crisp.

What helped me make the decision to attempt to quit smoking is some news I heard the other night at the baseball game.

I was sitting next to Sports Editor Jesse Outlar, who smokes, and he was telling me Henry Aaron had quit smoking.

"He smoked all those years he was playing ball every day," said Jesse, "and then when he's retired, he decides to give up smoking. If he had quit fifteen years ago, he might have hit a thousand home runs."

But it is more difficult for a writer to quit smoking than for anybody else because smoking sort of goes with writing. I would normally have another cigarette about here while pausing to figure out how to end this piece, which is now into the home stretch.

I think what I will do is type just as fast as I can because thisis a boutto driveme crayz, If I couldhave a cigaretteer ight xxx right now, I notonly would smokeit, I would eat thefil ter.

Ithas also occurred tome thatif I xxx reallyhad to have a ciagrette, xxxI couldgo a head and smoooooke itand who would knowthe difference?

Inother words, I could lieabout this whole thing andwrite how I got through thiscolumn without having a cigar xxxxette, and have allthe cigarxx ettes Iwanted to becasueyou can't seeme whil Iam writing this.

Trust me.

A Case
of the
Cutes

*I am always looking for ways to serve the
public. Here, I discuss one of the average
citizen's greatest problems: How to tell whose
restroom is whose in a restaurant. Please read
carefully.*

historians may look back to the current period of
American life and call it our "cute" phase and wonder what
happened to all the adults.

We are all driving cute little cars with funsie little names,
"Rabbit" and "Pinto" and "Sunbird." Blow their cute little horns
and hear the cute little sound: "Beep! Beep!"

We read cute little magazines like *People* and *Us*, and we
watch cute little television programs starring cute little people
with cute little names like "Mork" and "Mindy."

Imagine trying   to carry on an intelligent, grownups
conversation with somebody named "Mork" or "Mindy." I'd
rather try to talk to the air filter on a Pinto station wagon.

We also dress in cute little clothes nowadays, jeans and
T-shirts and orange sneakers, and we wear them to do cute things
like go roller skating.

Bleech!

We even have a "cutie" running for president. He is Jerry
Brown, the governor of California. He even thinks he has a
chance to win.

150

How cute.

Restaurants are the worst offenders, however. They have gone "cute crazy." Clowns serve hamburgers and waiters are in pirate suits, and the menu is printed on a balloon you can keep.

Restaurants also serve cute dishes. "Happy Meals" in a box. Seafood restaurants serve "Cap'n's Delight," which is crab meat with hollandaise, and the bottom of the plate has real barnacles.

Zowie, what fun!

You can also get all sorts of darling little drinks before you eat in a restaurant. Piña coladas, apricot daiquiris, rum and Dr. Pepper.

Also, there are those precious little green bottles with nothing but water inside that fuzz-brains drink.

Restaurants have even gotten cute with their restrooms. That makes me very angry. Going to the restroom is a serious matter, and it should be kept as simple as possible.

It used to be that when you went to a restroom in a restaurant, all you had to do was ask directions and then find the door marked "men" or "women" or in spiffy places, "ladies" or "gentlemen." You chose the appropriate door and then walked through it to take care of your needs.

That has all changed. Restaurant restrooms are no longer marked plainly "men" or "women" or "ladies" or "gentlemen." Go into a restaurant that serves Mexican food. The restroom doors will be marked "senors" or "senoritas." If the management is really into "cute," they may be marked, "muchachos" and "muchachas."

It's the same for other restaurants that serve ethnic foods. If you don't speak the language, you could be in trouble.

I suppose people with at least a fair amount of intelligence can usually select the correct restroom in those instances, but there are occasions when the choices are not that clear.

151

Watch yourself in restaurants that specialize in fried chicken. They often use "roosters" and "hens" on their restroom doors.

I happen to know the difference. I am "rooster." But I have an advantage. As a child, one of my chores was to gather the eggs from the henhouse. You pick up who's what in chickens rather quickly that way.

Others might not be so fortunate as to have that background, however, and there is nothing quite so embarrassing as strolling unannounced into the wrong roost.

I could go on, but I don't want to lose any more of my temper. It is simply time grownups started demanding grownup products and grownup services.

If for no other reason, there is too much else for an adult to worry about today to have to go through potty training again.

Don't laugh. Been in one of those western steak houses lately? Some western steak houses don't even bother with names on their restroom doors. They just have pictures of cowboys and cowgirls.

Whom do you favor more. Roy or Dale?

Careful, Tex. They both wore boots, you know.

7
Violence:
Five Victims

Officer
Frank
Schlatt

*Frank Schlatt was a good cop who was blown
away in the line of duty. His daughter must be
nearly grown by now. And the man who shot
him probably doesn't have that long before he is
eligible for parole.*

to the man who shot Frank Robert Schlatt:

You should have been there Tuesday morning. You should
have been there at the funeral service they held for your victim.

Was it easy to pull that trigger? Was it easy to point that
sawed-off shotgun at Frank Robert Schlatt and shoot him in the
face?

What happened? Did you panic? You and your accomplices
were robbing a furniture store. In walked Officer Frank Robert
Schlatt of the Atlanta Police Department. You shot him. Three
hours later, he was dead.

I want to tell you about the funeral, and I pray to God you
read this. You should know about the pain, the heartbreak, the
grief you caused.

Officer Schlatt was thirty-one. He was only thirty-one. It's

155

like the priest said Tuesday morning. "How can we explain death when it occurs in the midst of a life with so much potential unfulfilled?" Could you have explained that Tuesday morning?

It was a beautiful spring day. The chapel out in Forest Park was packed with people. That many again waited outside.

You have probably been to a funeral before. You probably know how haunting organ music in the background can be. As the people filed into the chapel, the organ was playing "The Battle Hymn of the Republic."

A number of important people came. The mayor was there, along with commissioners and ex-commissioners and even an ex-governor, Lester Maddox. He sat alone to pay his respects to the man you killed.

There were flowers everywhere. There was even a police badge made of white and blue flowers.

Policemen from all over came to mourn Officer Schlatt. They came from as far away as Phenix City, Alabama. One would tell me, "When a fellow officer dies, it's like something inside you dying. It is infuriating."

You know what he said about you? He said: "I don't see how that killer can live with his conscience . . . if he has a conscience."

An honor guard brought in the casket. Three members of the honor guard had worked all-night shifts, but volunteered to be at the funeral Tuesday morning. That is how they felt about the man you killed.

The priest said something I wish you could have heard. He was talking about death not being final. Officer Schlatt, he said, "was a good man. And you cannot bury a good man."

The casket was bronze. It was draped with an American flag. The honor guard marched in. They wore white hats and white gloves. As the services continued, two members of the guard

156

stood at strict attention on either side of the casket. One was white. One was black.

"These men fight among themselves all the time," said a man who is paid to monitor the police department, "but at a time like this, they all come together."

That should worry you. They will find you and bring you to justice. You can count on it.

I wish you could have been standing with me outside when they brought Officer Schlatt's body from the chapel.

Scripture was read. There was a prayer. The family sat under a tent in folding chairs, just a few feet from the one they loved so much.

There was Office Schlatt's father. He gazed ahead in shock and disbelief. There was his mother, a tiny, graying lady who wept openly. Another relative fainted.

There was also the widow. She wore black, her shoulders covered in a white shawl. I watched her as she tried to say The Lord's Prayer aloud. She choked on every word. She was such a pretty woman, even in her grief. She was blonde and small. Young widows can break the coldest heart. Maybe even yours.

I wish you could have seen the honor guard fold the flag. Their leader broke down. I wish you could have seen the mayor hand the flag to Office Schlatt's widow. I wish you could have heard the bugler blow taps.

More than anything, I wish you could have seen your victim's daughter. She is twelve. Her name is Jodie. She cried, too. She cried hard and she cried long.

There was a small flower on top of the casket. It was red and white. When the honor guard folded the flag, they folded the flower inside it.

It was Jodie's flower. She had placed it on her daddy's casket.

You should have been there.

Two
Good
Soldiers

Islamabad, Pakistan. December, 1979. A group
of screaming idiots attack and burn the United
States Embassy. Brian Ellis and Steven
Crowley, two American servicemen, are killed.
Lest we forget.

Citizens have been complaining about the American
servicemen who were released as hostages from the United States
Embassy in Iran.

They are complaining because the soldiers accepted their
releases.

"What kind of men do we have in our armed services today?"
a reader asked in a letter to the newspaper.

"Those released from the embassy in Iran should have
refused to leave and stayed on to protect the others and to show
Iran the American military has the guts and fortitude to stick out
any situation."

People who write letters like that have mush for brains.

One, it is rather doubtful that the young soldiers had any
choice in the matter.

Two, what could they have realistically accomplished by
staying, other than making a few mushbrains back home "feel
proud to be Americans?"

Three, if there is so much concern about the courage and
integrity of American servicemen, why doesn't somebody write

something in the newspaper about the two soldiers at our embassy in Islamabad, Pakistan, who also came home recently?

In boxes.

It's been only two weeks since they died. Would one in a thousand Americans even remember their names?

Brian Ellis, an army warrant officer, died in Islamabad. He was thirty. They found his charred remains in the rubble that was the embassy after the attack.

The exact details of his death aren't known, but a Baptist minister in his hometown of Spring Lake, North Carolina, said Brian Ellis "loved his country and the army. He was committed to the defense of his country."

That is at least a hint that he died trying to protect American lives and American property.

Marine Cpl. Steven Crowley also died in Islamabad, one day after the second anniversary of his Marine Corps enlistment.

He was twenty. The posthumous Bronze Star citation he was awarded included what details the Marine Corps knows about his death.

When the attack came, Corporal Crowley took his post on the roof of the embassy. He was immediately exposed to a barrage of rocks and whatever else the attackers could find to throw, as well as small-arms fire.

He never budged. He was able to give valuable information to those on the inside, and he was able to act as a diversion to buy time for them to reach the safety of the embassy security vault.

A man at Marine headquarters in Washington told me over the telephone, "Corporal Crowley got it in the head. We don't know if he was shot or if he was hit by a flying missile. We do know, however, it was pretty bad. There was some debate about whether to open the casket at his funeral."

Steven Crowley was one of nine children. After his father died, said those who knew him, Steven Crowley helped support his mother and younger brothers and sisters, even when he was in high school.

He was a good Catholic. He was a member of his high school track team. He was on the staff of his high school newspaper. He was an expert cabinet maker. He worked to keep classmates away from drugs.

After his death, his hometown church in Port Jefferson, New York, carried an insert in the Sunday morning worship program, giving other details of Steven Crowley's life. The insert included these words: "He was a thoughtful young man who was personally concerned with the well-being of others."

The reader was worried about what kind of men we have in our armed services today.

I can't answer that, except to say that now there are two less damn good ones.

160

Morris
Galanti

*The problem with writing about murder in a
big city is you could write the same thing every
day. Just change the names. God help us.*

the Atlanta police officers at the scene Tuesday morning,
the beginning of a bright autumn day, were not in a pleasant
mood. They were investigating a robbery murder that had taken
place the day before.

Two men had robbed King's Food Market at 559 Boulevard
N. E., a small grocery store that catered to lower income
customers. Morris S. Galanti, who was fifty-seven, had been in
business at that location for fifteen years.

"I thought the world of him," said a man standing outside the
store. "It tore me up when I heard what happened. I did all my
business with him."

What really did happen is still mostly a matter of speculation.
Police think Morris Galanti may have been forced to lie
face-down on the floor near one of his cash registers while the
robbery was taking place. At least that is where and how they
found him.

With a bullet in his back. He died later at Grady Hospital.

One officer was talking about what might be the mood of the
killer now. That is apparently important in order to determine
what might be his subsequent actions following the crime.

"I'll bet he thinks he's big . . . now," said the office. "He's
killed a man."

161

"If we could break out the rubber hoses," said another, "we might could put a stop to things like this."

"Scumbags," said a third policeman. "That's what we are dealing with here. Dirty, rotten scumbags."

These things happen all the time in a big city, you tell yourself. Neighborhood grocery stores are prime targets for robberies.

The papers report them the next day, but they are rarely page-one news, and soon another victim has been recorded. A couple of blocks down the street, much less across town, who even notices?

Sgt. H. W. McConnell of homicide was in the store Tuesday morning. He has seen his share of such waste of human life. He finally walked out of the store to the street and leaned against his car.

"Look at the wreath on the door," he said. "Isn't that something? A man works fifteen years and all that's here today to symbolize it is a damn green wreath."

He remembered a similar incident two blocks up the street six years before. An old man had been shot in his shoe store.

"I rode to Grady with him," he said. "Before he died, he could talk a little. I asked him who shot him. He said, 'Man did . . . Man did.' " I said, "I know a man shot you, but who was it?"

"We finally found out they called the one who shot him 'Man.' His dying words gave us what we needed."

There have been no such breaks in the case of Morris Galanti.

"There was a lot of animosity toward the ones who did this when we got here Monday," said Sgt. McConnell, "but it's still hard to get people to talk. They either don't want to get involved or they feel bitterness for the police, too."

How, I wanted to know, can storekeepers avoid losing their lives during a robbery attempt? Should they attempt to stop the robbery? What did Morris Galanti do wrong?

"He didn't do anything wrong. That's the hell of it," said Sgt. D. V. Lee. "But don't ever argue with a man with a gun, and don't ever resist him. Just give him everything he wants. He doesn't have that much to lose by killing you.

"And remember one thing: You can get more money, but you can't get another life."

Good advice. But the wreath, the green wreath on the door to Morris Galanti's store, had already said that.

Patti
Barry

I was very angry when I wrote this column. After it was completed, I had second thoughts about running it in the newspaper. Maybe I had gone too far, I said to myself.

But then I thought of Patti Barry again. So young. So pretty. So full of life. It was her birthday, and some street goon gunned her down.

The column received more favorable reaction than anything I have ever written. The letters and calls numbered in the thousands. Not because I said anything new, but because I said what the people were thinking.

In fact, the only negative call I received came from a guy over at City Hall, the mayor's press secretary.

it is four-thirty in the afternoon as I write this. My deadline is approaching. I will never make it. Let 'em wait a couple of minutes. What I have to say, I have to say. Not for the editors. Not even for you, the readers. But for myself.

I love this city. I left it once. I missed it harder than anything I have ever missed in my life.

I have cried like a baby twice as an adult. Once when I left Atlanta because I knew I had made a mistake, and once when I returned because I knew I had finally rectified it.

But this city is going to hell. It may already be there.

I don't care what the mayor says. The mayor is more concerned about his future political ambitions than the welfare of the citizens of this city.

I don't care what the Chamber of Commerce says. The Chamber of Commerce looks and sees dollar signs.

I don't care what the big-dog police commissioners say. They are the mayor's puppets.

This city is going to hell because you can get yourself killed walking its streets in broad daylight.

The details are elsewhere in this newspaper. Quickly, her name was Patricia Barry. She was twenty-six. She worked for a law firm.

It was her birthday. She and a friend were walking the streets of Atlanta at noon. They were walking to lunch to celebrate Patricia Barry's birthday.

At Peachtree and Forsyth—I walk there nearly every day—a goon shot Patricia Barry dead. "Just shot her," said her friend.

Then, the goon shot himself. He died, the coward.

Patricia Barry was the 185th homicide victim in Atlanta in 1979. My God, we've got two-and-one-half months to go.

What is wrong with this city is downtown is a zoo. A *zoo*. A month ago, I took an hour's walk from 72 Marietta Street down and around Central City Park and back to 72 Marietta Street again.

Drunks and punks were everywhere. Drunks and punks get crazy. They get mean. They rob. They steal. They kill.

Why doesn't somebody get the drunks and punks off the streets of Atlanta?

Why doesn't somebody, like the governor, order the state patrol back? Why doesn't somebody, like the governor, put a trooper on every corner in downtown until we can go an entire week without a citizen getting blown away?

Why doesn't somebody, like the governor, order the national guard in, if that is what it takes, to make this city safe again?

I am sick of Maynard Jackson. Maynard Jackson complains this newspaper overreacts to the city's increasing crime rate.

Call me, Maynard. I am overreacting to the point my hands are shaking.

I am sick of Lee Brown and George Napper. Let them tell Patricia Barry's family and friends, like they tell the rest of us, about the terrific job they are doing.

The Atlanta Journal carried the first story about Wednesday's downtown murder. Near the end of the article was a sentence that read, "The shooting was sure to revive controversy over the safety of downtown streets."

"Controversy"? What "controversy"? You mean there are those who would still question the fact there is a war zone down here?

That is exactly what we have on the streets of Atlanta. A war. The drunks and the punks against the rest of us.

And we're losing, goddammit. We're losing.

166

8

Critic-at-Large

"Dallas": Pass the Trash

I heard from a lot of other "Dallas" fans after writing this. One even sent me a bumper sticker. It read, "Free Sue Ellen."

i stumbled into my very first episode of the television hit, "Dallas," the other evening. I really don't know what I expected.

It sounded like a western—gunfights and a lot of horses and somebody is always getting hanged—but westerns rode off into the televison sunset years ago.

Maybe it was quiz show. Guess how high a Dallas Cowboys cheerleader can count, and win a weekend at the Fish or Cut Bait Dude Ranch near Tyler.

Or perhaps it was another cop series. Sort of a cow-town version of "CHIPS," which, incidentally, is a cowchip version of Broderick Crawford's old "Highway Patrol," ten-four.

"Dallas" turned out to be none of the above. It is a prime-time soap opera—who's pregnant this week?—and what do you think about that, buckaroos?

Previously, only housewives and lazy scoundrels who

wouldn't work could watch soap operas because soap operas were never shown after dark.

But with "Dallas" comes the opportunity for the rest of us to get in on the fun, even the kids, who can learn a lot watching the program, like the intelligence of adults is probably vastly overrated.

"Dallas" is a CBS production, the same network that gives us Walter Cronkite. It sits high atop the Nielsen ratings. It appears on Friday nights at ten o'clock, nine o'clock central. Check your local listings if you live somewhere it gets late earlier.

In case you have missed "Dallas" so far, don't worry. A soap opera is like a large plate of cold, boiled rutabagas. Even if you start in the middle, you haven't missed a thing.

I can, however, offer you considerable background after viewing just one episode.

"Dallas" involves the trials and tribulations of the Ewing family of Southfork Ranch, which is located a short hop in the ol' Mercedes from downtown "Big D."

There is Jock Ewing, the head of the family, who got filthy rich in shady oil dealings. He is played by Jim Davis, who used to play "Railroad Detective" and whose face looks like it finished second in a pick-axe fight.

His wife is Miss Ellie, who seems like a nice person, but we will probably find out she doesn't shave her legs and spends a curious amount of time hanging out at rodeos.

There is J. R., number one son. J. R. runs the family business now. You wouldn't trust J. R. in the same room with your Doberman.

Sue Ellen is J. R.'s wife. Bobby is J. R.'s brother. Pam is his wife. Lucy is his cute, little blonde niece, who is bound to get involved in something just awful because she's built like a brick hay barn and has that look about her.

J. R. and Sue Ellen have a lousy marriage, so J. R. is

170

sleeping with Kristin, Sue Ellen's sister. Sue Ellen is no fool. Sue Ellen, somebody said, used to ride the range with Pam's brother, Cliff, but now she has roped a cowboy, whose name escapes me, ooh-la-la.

Bobby, meanwhile, has something going with an old childhood sweetheart, but you can't blame him for that because Pam went to Paris with her boss for the weekend.

Confused? You should be. "It would take a motelkeeper to know who was in what bed in the Ewing family, and why," said *Time* magazine of the "Dallas" plots and subplots.

Utter trash is what I say of "Dallas." Sex, sex, and more sex. The fact "Dallas" sits high atop the Nielsen ratings is further proof our television tastebuds are located south of where they were originally intended.

If "Dallas" were a movie, it would be rated "R." For "rotten."

If it were a sport, it would be love wrestling.

And if I miss tonight's episode, I'll die.

The Demise of Drive-Ins

There are still a few drive-in movies around, but they're not packed like they were in the old days. It is a shame an entire generation of Americans will grow up having never had to learn their way around the back seat of a 1957 Chevrolet.

bang the drum slowly. An institution passes from our midst. The obituary appeared in last week's newspaper. Drive-in movie theaters, the article said, are goners.

For years, I thought drive-in theaters were for watching movies out-of-doors. Then I went to one with Kathy Sue Loudermilk, bless her heart. She was a lovely child and a legend before her sixteenth birthday. She was twenty-one, however, before she knew an automobile had a front seat.

Dressed in something tight, Kathy Sue could have stopped traffic at the Indianapolis 500. When she graduated from high school, they retired her sweater.

The last time I was at a drive-in theater, come to think of it, it was with Kathy Sue. I forget what was playing. I remember it didn't matter in the least.

You had to be careful at our drive-in because of the theater patrolman, Hascal "The Rascal" Pitts. Hascal's favorite thing was to slip behind a seemingly abandoned car and surprise the couple inside with his flashlight, the biggest and brightest the hardware store had to offer.

172

"Ah, ha!" he would scream in delight at his discoveries. On a busy night, Hascal could run through an entire set of batteries before the end of the second feature.

Hascal did have a tough job, but he was paid well for his efforts. He got twenty-five dollars a week and all he could see.

Drive-ins have been going downhill steadily. That much was obvious when the motel industry boomed. Now they have motels with adult movies inside the rooms. That seems a waste. Once the door is locked and the curtains are drawn, most couples don't need an instructional film.

There are people, I suppose, who go to drive-ins simply to watch the movies, and they have gone low-budget, low-quality.

Macon County Line was a drive-in biggie. So was *Return to Macon County Line*. All seven *Walking Talls* played at drive-ins, and *Saturday Night Fever* should have if it didn't.

I checked the current drive-in features in the Atlanta area this week. Wonder why nobody goes to drive-ins anymore? Check this line-up:

- *Tintorera—Tiger Shark*. Another *Jaws* spin-off, filmed in one afternoon in the producer's bathtub. Stars Susan George, Fiona Lewis, Jennifer Ashley, Hugo Tiglitz, and Andres Garcia as a rubber duck gone berserk.

- *Eaten Alive*. Spin-off of *Tintorera—Tiger Shark*. Stars Susan George, Fiona Lewis, Jennifer Ashley, Hugo Tiglitz, and Andres Garcia, who should turn in overtime.

- *Chain Gang Women*. Wrenching story of lust in rural prison camp. Rated "S" for "stinks."

- *Buckstone County Prison*. Wrenching story of lust in rural prison camp. Rated "R" for "ripoff."

- *The Tool Box Murder*. Stars Cameron Mitchell, Pamelyn Ferdin, Wesley Eure, and Andres Garcia as the tool box. Intriguing drama on how to wipe out an entire neighborhood using only a Phillips-head screwdriver and four tacks.

● *Starship Invasion*. Cousin of *Close Encounters*. Greyhound bus stops in Moultrie, Georgia, and strange creature emerges. Turns out it's only Hickey Bates, local druggist, in his new beige leisure suit he picked up on sale in Macon.

A Zillion Light Years from Virginia City

"Battlestar Galactica" didn't turn out to be a smash hit, and the last time I saw Lorne Greene, he was back down to earth in his cowboy boots selling dog food.

this is the week for television's fall premieres. This is also the week the television industry should be made to take the first moon shuttle out of town.

The new shows don't concern me that much. I am too disappointed some of the old ones are back. "Starsky and Hutch," for instance. I can never remember which one is Starsky and which one is Hutch, but I do think they make a cute couple.

I would like to see a combination episode of some of the old programs. Say, "Starsky and Hutch" with "Laverne and Shirley." What happens is, Starsky and Hutch pistol-whip Laverne and Shirley during a Milwaukee drug bust and then are devoured themselves by a Channel 17 rerun of *The Blob*.

The new fall rage is supposed to be a space adventure called "Battlestar Galactica" that premiered for three hours on ABC Sunday night. Three hours is a long time for anything to premiere. In fact, the only uncomfortable television program I have seen last longer is a Braves game.

Space adventure is hot because of the smashing box office of the movie *Star Wars*. I never saw *Star Wars*, but a friend of mine did.

175

"Saw it twice," he said. "Once straight and once stoned."

I think he meant the second time he saw *Star Wars*, he was somewhere out in space himself.

I tried the same tactic Sunday night while watching the premiere of "Battlestar Galactica." I was high on a plate of butterbeans.

Space adventure is nothing new on television. In my youth, we had "The Adventures of Flash Gordon," starring Buster Crabbe, the famous swimmer.

Flash Gordon wore a Peter Pan outfit and battled the evil Ming, who was uglier than both Laverne and Shirley and meaner than Starsky and Hutch beating up a drunk in the park.

What Flash did mostly was save Dr. Zarkov's semi-beautiful daughter—I forget her name—from Ming's soldiers, all of whom looked like tree stumps with beards.

After viewing the opening segment of "Battlestar Galactica," I contend nothing much has changed about television space adventure.

You've seen one television spaceship, you've seen them all. Flash Gordon toured the heavens in something that looked like empty pork-and-bean cans covered in aluminum foil, and so did the cast of "Battlestar Galactica."

And the highlight of any space adventure is still a ray-gun battle. Ray guns make people disappear instead of blowing holes in them. If Starsky and Hutch had ray guns, their programs wouldn't be nearly as bloody, and kids wouldn't have to stay up so late to watch them.

I am conceding "Battlestar Galactica" had a plot, but it was difficult to follow. A group of people-people were involved in a deadly conflict with reptile-people and grasshopper-people and machine-people. The machine-people looked like what you might do with the rest of the empty pork-and-bean cans and a couple of leftover rolls of aluminum foil.

176

What upset me most about "Battlestar Galactica" was who played the head human. Lorne Greene. The last time I saw Lorne Greene, he was petting a puppy on a dog food commercial.

Sunday night, he stood behind the controls of the "Battlestar Galactica," a zillion light years from Virginia City.

Lorne Greene, who ran the grandest ranch in all of Nevada, who was "Pa" to Little Joe and Hoss, who fought outlaws and Indians and anything else the western wilds could throw at him, wore a black dress and a jeweled necklace.

I suppose a good actor can make any sort of transition, but it is a blessing, I was thinking, Hoss didn't live to see his daddy dressed up like a dance hall girl.

Tom Snyder, by Golly

"Prime Time Sunday" later became "Prime Time Saturday," which improved the show greatly because I'm never home to watch television on Saturday nights.

the big news in television is now there is somebody else to hate and say nasty things about besides Howard Cosell of ABC. He is NBC's Tom Snyder, who has bushy eyebrows and goes around saying, "By golly."

Frankly, Tom Snyder may have pushed Howard Cosell all the way to second place as the television personality who makes the most viewers sick to their stomachs.

Nobody does Howard Cosell impressions at parties anymore. Now, everybody is doing Tom Snyder impressions. He's much easier to do than Cosell.

You sit in a chair at one o'clock in the morning, light a cigarette, and say something stupid.

Cosell could not be reached for comment on the dramatic developments, but a representative at ABC in New York did quash the rumor that Cosell, missing since late December, was recently eaten alive by the defensive unit of the Pittsburgh Steelers at a banquet in McKeesport.

Tom Snyder has been on television hosting talk shows and giving the news for a long time in cities like Milwaukee, Savannah, Atlanta, Philadelphia, Los Angeles, and New York.

Mostly, he has been on television so late at night that small children and normal people had better sense than to stay up and watch him.

So much for small blessings. Besides his nightly "Tomorrow" appearances where he interviews himself, Tom Snyder is now available for viewing on Sunday evenings during prime time. NBC is calling the new show "Prime Time Sunday." They have some real thinkers at NBC.

"Prime Time Sunday" is NBC's answer to the ever-popular CBS program, "60 Minutes." That's like answering a Russian Backfire bomber with a Messerschmidt armed with water balloons.

NBC even had the shameless audacity to hire Mike Wallace's kid for its "PTS" show. Mike Wallace, the star of "60 Minutes," is a Doberman pinscher. Unfortunately, his son Chris has all the forceful technique of a cocker spaniel puppy.

In many ways, Tom Snyder and Howard Cosell are alike. They are both arrogant and oft putrescent, and they use too many big words.

But Tom Snyder is more dangerous than Cosell. He involves himself in serious topics like our gasoline shortage and religious nuts begging money at airports.

All Cosell ever does is ramble on about the Dallas punter's hang time.

I watched Tom Snyder perform during his first two "Prime Time Sunday" programs. I wanted to hit him in the mouth.

He also had dumb shows. He sits in front of a large screen and talks to people from somewhere in Canada and Decatur, Illinois, who are nervous and don't know exactly what to say or when to say it.

They also perspire a greal deal. An NBC biography of Tom Snyder says he has "shown a remarkable ability to illuminate issues and personalities." It doesn't say anything about his

179

remarkable ability to make some poor stiff standing in a Canadian oil field sweat like a racehorse.

There was also a "Prime Time Sunday" segment where the program unveiled the earthshaking information that Americans were planning to do a lot of camping on the Fourth of July. It was a thirty-second bit. Unfortunately, it lasted eleven minutes.

But there are usually two sides to every story. There must be something nice that can be said for Tom Snyder.

There is. I decided long ago what this country needs desperately to do is let Elvis Presley rest in peace and quit complaining about Howard Cosell.

Nobody has released a tribute-to-the-King record in months, and Tom Snyder has taken our minds off Howard Cosell.

By golly, that's the best news since Phyllis George disappeared.

"... And Now
for the
Weather ... "

*If local television news were an animal, it would
be a duck.*

—Old Journalism School Saying.

i was watching the local television news program the other
evening, and a man walked onto the screen and talked for nearly
five minutes about the weather. *For nearly five minutes.*

Television news has done it again, I said to myself. Gone slap
overboard.

I can recall when the entire local television news program
lasted only fifteen minutes. "President Eisenhower said
today . . . ," and what followed was quick and concise.

No would-be clever repartee between the anchor person and
his underlings. No "live-action" reports from the site of an
afternoon fender-bender.

You got the news, a few ball scores, and then out came a man
in a baggy suit with the weather report. He drew a few raindrops
and snowflakes and happy suns on a big map and said, "Today, it
will rain. Tomorrow, it won't."

That was the weather report. That was enough.

But local television news is always looking for a better way to
do something that was fine in the first place. So Baggy Suit was
eventually canned, and what followed him was the smiling
"weathergirlperson."

"And what can I do for you, young lady?" asked the station manager.

"I want to be a smiling weathergirlperson," said the sensuous blonde, crossing her legs.

"Can you draw raindrops and snowflakes and happy suns?" the station manager probed.

"No, but I'm a fast learner," replied the blonde.

"You're hired," said the station manager.

So for years, we got our television weather reports from smiling weathergirlpersons.

"What's the weather for tomorrow, Bonnie Sue?" asked the eleven o'clock anchor man.

"A tornado will touch down at noon and wipe out half the city," answered Bonnie Sue, smiling.

But even that approach to television weather is dying. What stations, especially those in major markets, are doing today is hiring full-fledged, card-carrying meteorologists to give the weather, and their forecasts all have the stamp of approval of the American Meteorological Society, which sounds important even if it probably doesn't mean diddly.

The fellow I watched the other evening was one of the new breed of television weathermen. He had all the latest equipment.

He had color radar. He had satellite photos. He gave me the latest information on upper-atmosphere air currents.

He talked about "anomalous propagation," which sounded like something that should be performed only by consenting adults and only behind closed doors, and then he gave a long-range forecast that will last me from now to Groundhog Day.

I don't need that much. I don't want it. I don't understand it. Unless you happen to be a moose, who really cares if a high-pressure system is building over Saskatchewan?

All that Fancy-smancy weather reporting has taken away the mystery of the weather, the anticipation of it. We may as well forget the *Farmer's Almanac* and ignore the old man whose arthritis hasn't missed a rainstorm in fifty years.

Local television news has a basic problem. Because of its competitive nature and because people involved in television apparently do little thinking, it must constantly figure ways to combine show business with some occasional journalism.

That is what brought us giggling weather girls. That is what has now brought us weather reports that are too long and too complicated. That is what will eventually bring us television weather forecasts when somebody will walk out and *sing*.

The Painful
Stigma of
Roller Skates

This is a good story to read to your children on Christmas. It teaches a number of lessons, including humility, which is an important trait to learn or somebody might bash in your head with a roller skate.

a new movie is out called *Skatetown USA*, and people are flocking to see it because of the recent surge of interest in roller-skating.

I haven't seen the movie, but I have seen the advertisements in the newspaper which show a handsome boy skating with a pretty girl who isn't exactly dressed for cool and damp weather.

All sorts of big-time groups like Earth, Wind and Fire; The Jacksons; and Heatwave, provide the music for the movie; and I suppose what the movie does is portray dancing and skating on wheels as the latest chic activity of the beautiful people.

So maybe it is, but I do want to offer the reminder that roller-skating wasn't the recent brainchild of some Perrier-swilling promotor looking for a way to get the jet set out of their Jacuzzis.

Roller-skating, history tells us, has its roots deep in the nation's poor households, where Christmas was always a low-budget holiday.

When I was growing up, you could always tell the financial status of the community's families by what the kids got for Christmas.

Well-to-do kids, like Alvin Bates, got bicycles, Erector sets, and air guns for Christmas. Poor kids got roller skates.

Roller-skating, I can imagine, was probably invented by some down-and-out-of-work mechanic who didn't have money for his children's Christmas, so he worked for weeks by candlelight in the dank basement of his three-room house until he had roughed out the first likeness of roller skates for Barney, Shirley, and little Joey.

Now, roller skates cost an arm and a leg, and stars like Cher are performing on them, and little Joey's old man didn't get a dime out of it.

I got roller skates for Christmas for six straight years. So did my boyhood friend and idol, Weyman C. Wannamaker, Jr., a great American.

After returning to school from Christmas holidays, the teacher would always put us through the torturous exercise in which everybody would stand and tell what he or she got for Christmas.

Alvin Bates was always first because he always sat at the front of the room.

"I got a bicycle, an Erector set, and an air gun," he would announce, smirking at the roller-skate segment of the classroom.

"And what did you get, Weyman?" the teacher would ask.

"I'll give you a hint," Weyman would answer. "What has eight wheels, two leather straps, and still costs a lousy three bucks at the hardware store?"

Those were terrible times, but there was one glorious moment I can still recall as if it were yesterday. Soon after Christmas in the seventh grade, Alvin Bates made the terribly stupid mistake of riding past Weyman's house on his new bicycle.

Weyman took it as a personal insult and donned his skates and rolled off in hot pursuit. Color Weyman gone on a pair of roller skates. He caught up in less than three blocks and took off

185

one of his skates and beat large and painful knots on Alvin's head with it.

So let them disco the night away on roller skates in *Skatetown USA*. Let the bright lights shine, and let the music play.

I will rest in the knowledge it was the poor people who pioneered roller-skating in this country, and it was Weyman C. Wannamaker, Jr., a great American, who long ago struck the blow for those of us who had to bear the stigma of poverty that roller-skating once carried.

The scene remains so vivid in my mind: Alvin Bates sitting on the curb, holding his aching, bleeding head and crying, and Weyman, filled with sweet revenge, skating away into a hurrying sundown.

Who needs a roller-skating movie when you have already sat in on roller-skating history?

9

Stray Dogs and
Sweet Memories

The "Marvelous" Le Fevres

After she read this, Eva Mae Le Fevre called me and said if I would drop by sometime she would play me an old gospel song. I've got that down as one of the things I absolutely must do before I die.

i grew up on gospel music, and Sunday mornings have never been the same since there was no more gospel music on the radio to dress for church by.

I'm talking about Hovie Lister's kind of gospel music. And Leroy Abernathy and Shorty Bradford—"The Happy Two"—and a group my daddy loved, The Le Fevres.

You put somebody at a piano, and the sound that emerges is almost rinky-tink. The tall fellow in the back sings a deep, hollow bass, and his short, cherubic friend on the end takes over the high parts.

Gospel music now, I gather, has gone big-time and rhinestone, and send $10.95 for a framed picture of *The Last Supper* that glows in the dark.

I found the obituary in the back pages of the paper last week.

189

I suppose a two-column headline on an obit says the deceased achieved at least some notoriety during his lifetime, but to send Urias Le Fevre away without even a picture seemed an oversight.

He was sixty-nine, and he died last Wednesday of cancer. He spent fifty-four years of his life singing gospel music. And there was even more to him than that.

I talked to one of his neighbors a couple of hours before the funeral Thursday. The neighbor said, "He was a good man, a good father to his children, and a good husband to Eva Mae."

What memories I have. It is Sunday afternoon and the lunch dishes have been cleared away, and supper will be what chicken wasn't eaten and a cold biscuit, if you're lucky. It is the early days of television.

We watched westerns and we watched wrestling matches. And Sunday afternoons, we watched and listened to The Le Fevres.

Eva Mae at the piano. Urias and his brother Alphus in perfect harmony. Only the deaf could resist tapping a toe.

"Marvelous," my father would say, as only he could say it, "absolutely marvelous."

I can even remember the commercials. God bless Martha White Flour for bringing the music of The Le Fevres to my childhood.

Theirs was one of the most successful gospel-singing television shows ever. The show was live for years, but videotape later made it possible for the Le Fevres to syndicate to sixty-five other stations across the nation.

It all began for brothers Urias and Alphus before their teens, when they would sing about the Lord with their sister Maude, back home in Tennessee.

Urias Le Fevre's obituary last week said the group turned down many offers to leave gospel music and go into the more

190

lucrative field of country-western music. The Le Fevres weren't interested; they saw their musical talents as a "Christian calling."

The senior members of the Le Fevre group, Urias, Alphus and Eva Mae, retired a couple of years ago. They had a million miles and a million songs behind them. The younger members of the family are continuing, and one son, Mylon, sings rock 'n' roll.

"I think the family's already left for the funeral," said the neighbor last week as we talked. "I took a half-day off to go myself. Everybody in this neighborhood loved Urias."

But the neighbor had a little time. So he asked, "Want to hear something pretty?"

I didn't have to answer. He already had the record in his hand, and he placed it on the turntable. It was The Le Fevres, and they were singing "He Pilots My Ship."

We listened, and when it was over, I never hesitated with my reaction:

"Marvelous," I brought back from a long time ago, "absolutely marvelous."

191

Country Mudhole

Journalism students sometimes ask me, "Where do you get your ideas for columns?" They wouldn't believe me if I told them. Inspiration may be found in the strangest of places, even in muddy parking lots.

WStatesboro, Ga.

hat I happened to be doing in Statesboro has nothing to do with what is to follow. Let's just say Statesboro is one of my favorite stops in the hinterlands, and I have a buddy here who tells good stories and enjoys staying up late telling them.

What this is really all about is mudholes. My buddy and I were going to this place in Statesboro for lunch, and we pulled into the dirt parking lot, and in the middle of the parking lot was a good country mudhole, the likes of which I hadn't seen in years.

We don't have mudholes in the city. We have potholes. There is a difference. Potholes are synthetic. They are caused by cars and trucks driving over cheap asphalt and concrete, and they are a sorry thing that causes much cursing and even damage to the cars and trucks that drive into them.

Mudholes are real. I don't know what really causes mudholes but my guess is they are caused by God's rain hitting God's good earth, and I like that.

Mudholes, like potholes, can be ornery, too. Drive into one with a new wash job on your car, and so much for your new wash job. But anybody stupid enough to drive a just-washed car onto a dirt road where there are likely to be mudholes deserves what he gets.

192

But mudholes can also offer good times and much recreation. There was a big mudhole in the schoolyard of my youth. When it rained, it was days before the mudhole dried up.

During recess, it was great fun to entice a girl to stand near the mudhole and then throw a large rock into same, thus splashing mud and water all over her dress and shoes and face and hair.

This usually caused the girl to cry, except in the case of Cordie Mae Poovy, the meanest girl in school. Once, in a moment of insanity, I threw a rock into the mudhole and splashed Cordie Mae.

She ran me down on the ballfield and hit me in the mouth and then dragged me back to the mudhole and washed away my sins and the blood that covered my mouth.

Another time, I spotted my dog, Butch, wallowing in the mudhole in my front yard. I jumped in with Butch, clothes and all. My mother beat me for the remainder of the afternoon and through the early portion of the evening.

Butch, the scoundrel who instigated the entire affair, shook himself off and then curled up under my grandfather's truck and went to sleep.

There is one thing you can't do in a mudhole, however, and that is fish. People who fish in mudholes are a little fuzzy, which brings up the name of the legendary "Gums" Garfield, who hadn't had teeth since Roosevelt's second term.

Gums was more than a little fuzzy, and my boyhood friend and idol, Weyman C. Wannamaker, Jr., a great American, enjoyed playing tricks on him.

One day, Weyman said to Gums, "Hey, Gums, you like to fish?"

"I love to fish," replied Gums.

Weyman then explained to Gums about the big mudhole over behind the Baptist church.

193

"I caught a seven-pound catfish there last week," Weyman said.

Gums immediately went home and got his cane pole and hurried to the big mudhole behind the Baptist church. The preacher, preparing his Sunday sermon, watched Gums for a time from his study and finally could stand it no longer.

He walked out to the mudhole and said to Gums, "Who put you up to this?"

Gums told him.

"Don't you know he was just kidding you?" said the preacher. "There aren't any fish in a mudhole."

"I know that, preacher," replied Gums, as he pulled a clean hook out of the water. "That's why I wasn't using any bait."

I would like to dedicate this column to Cordie Mae, Butch, Weyman, Gums, and the preacher. Also, to my buddy down in Statesboro who bet me a lunch I couldn't write an entire column based on a country mudhole.

"Buddy"

*I get sentimental about dogs. I can't help it. If
you have ever looked deep into a dog's eyes and
felt he was urgently trying to give you a
message, then maybe you will understand what
I was feeling when I wrote the following.*

mOn a Back Road
y grandfather would have called the dog a
"sooner."

"Just as soon stay in the house as out," he would have
laughed.

The day was ending, but a long drive home remained. I had
stopped for gasoline in one of those all-purpose country service
stations, the kind where there is always a little boy with a dirty
face and a dog hanging around.

The little boy was buying milk for his mother. The dog was
yawning and scratching.

"That your dog?" I asked the old man pumping the gasoline.

"Took up here," he said.

"Fine-looking dog," I went on.

"Smart, too," said the man. "Watch this."

He locked the pump to "on" and walked over to the dog. He
held out his hand, and the dog responded by lifting a paw. Smart
as a whip, that dog.

"How long you had him?" I said.

" 'Bout a week," said the man.

"Any bother?"

"Not a bit. I figure somebody put him out of a car. That little
boy that was here buying the milk wants him, but his mama won't

195

let him bring the dog home. Says every dog he brings home gets run over, and it upsets the little boy something awful."

That was an instant memory. I had a losing streak with dogs, too.

There was "Snowball." Every child eventually gets a furry white dog named "Snowball." My daddy bought me mine the day after he got back from Korea. "Snowball" got it from a laundry truck.

"Butch" was later. He chased cars. One day, he caught one.

The vet said "Pokey" had pneumonia. He allowed me to pet my dog one last time, and then he took "Pokey" into a back room, and I never saw my dog again.

I had "Plato." Now there was a dog. I lost him in a divorce settlement, believe it or not. I gave up dogs after that. Missing a dog is a worrisome pain.

"This dog got a name?" I said to the man at the station.

"I call him 'Buddy.' "

The old man scratched the dog, and "Buddy" nuzzled close to the source of affection.

I petted the dog myself. He was obviously of a generous mix, a young dog with patches of white and yellow and black. I tried the paw trick, and "Buddy" responded on cue. Impressive.

I like dogs because they forgive easily, know little or nothing about revenge, and will settle for thirty seconds of care and attention if that is all you have to spare.

I have a house and it is empty, and I have considered adding a dog to the premises. But then I decided that is foolish because I often sleep where I fall, and I do not want a lonely dog on my conscience.

I paid the man for the gasoline and started to get back in my car. The dog was staring at me, or maybe it was just my imagination. Regardless, I stared back.

"You like that dog, don't you?" said the man, smiling.

"That's a fine dog," I said.

"Why don't you take him with you? I got another dog at home."

I gave him five or six excellent reasons why I couldn't and drove away.

It's been a week now. It was dark that night and I wasn't familiar with the road. I doubt I could ever find that country service station again, even if I wanted to.

Which, you understand, I don't.

Saturday Night Fever

News Item: The Ku Klux Klan is on the rise again.

not much exciting ever happened in my hometown after the trains on the Atlanta and West Point line quit stopping for passengers. This was rural Georgia, early fifties.

But then there was that one week of anticipation, of wonderment, of an amount of sheer terror for boys of eight and nine.

I can still see the posters somebody nailed to fence posts: "KLAN RALLY."
"SATURDAY NIGHT."
"STAND UP AND BE COUNTED."
"SAVE THE WHITE RACE."

I didn't understand, and neither did any of my friends. I asked my grandfather, the wisest person I knew.

"The Ku Klux Klan," he said, and he explained the best he could, with an unmistakable element of praise in his voice. The Ku Klux Klan, he said, was a sort of private police department.

You take a man who isn't making certain his wife and children have enough to eat, or a man who isn't working when there is work available, or a scoundrel who has left his fields unplowed to escape the sun in a beer joint, then the Klan, my grandfather explained, pays him a visit and suddenly he is more aware of his responsibilities as a father, husband, and citizen.

You don't pass off boyish curiosity that easily.

198

"What do they do to him?" I wanted to know.

"They flog him," said my grandfather.

"With what?"

I think he mentioned buggy whips and maybe leather straps. He said the visitations normally occurred after dark.

I didn't sleep very well that night. Nor the next, nor the next, because each day more information filtered down about what would happen Saturday night.

Those men, that "Klan," they wear hoods, somebody said. White hoods, with holes for their eyes and their mouths.

They burn crosses.

Sometimes, they burn people. The story was all about, unconcealed from the tenders who hung on every word. A black man—only nobody said "black man"—had been accused of something called "raping" a white woman up the road in the county seat some years before.

The Ku Klux Klan took care of him, the story went. They nailed his scrotum—only nobody said "scrotum"—to a stump and gave him a rusty razor blade and then set the stump on fire.

My grandfather said he doubted any such thing actually happened.

"You stay away from there Saturday night," my grandfather said.

Three of us, on bikes, were the first arrivals. We hid behind a clump of trees.

Spectators began piling in from all over, from as far away as LaGrange and even Columbus. They came in cars and on the backs of flat-bed trucks to an open field that was soon packed with humanity, or something that at least resembled it.

The three of us, we trembled when out of the darkened woods came a marching band of hooded men. Their torches lit the night.

They sang "Onward Christian Soldiers" as they marched.

The men aligned themselves shoulder-to-shoulder toward the crowd. One of the men stepped forward and began to speak about things my grandfather had not mentioned in his explanation. Race-mixing. Mongrelization, whatever that was. Nigger-this. Nigger-that.

An old man sat down front and said a lot of "Amens." Some older boys in the back were drinking something from a fruit jar.

When the speaker finished, the other hooded men set a torch to the ground, and a cross of flame erupted. The rally was closed with a prayer.

My grandfather was waiting for me when I returned home.

"You go to the Klan rally?" he asked.

I admitted my disobedience. It wasn't necessary. I was still shaking.

My grandfather took me into his arms. There was a long quiet. And then he said softly, but firmly, "Don't be afraid. Yellow cowards can't hurt you."

My grandfather, holding a frightened little boy and changing a long-held attitude, needed to hear himself say that, I think now, just as much as I did.

Ode to a Church Fan

After this column appeared in the newspaper, I received nearly a hundred church fans in the mail. This sort of work does have its benefits.

Somebody took a poll the other day concerning how Americans feel about going to church during these trying times, and the published results said the takers and the leavers were split something like 50-50.

I polled myself and decided I still enjoy going to church because it's OK to sing out on the choruses, but there are some things about the modern church that bother me.

In some churches, for instance, sermons are shortened during the football season so nobody will miss a one o'clock kickoff, and let us all stand and sing the first and third verses of "Drop Kick Me, Jesus, Through the Goalposts of Life," which, in case there are any doubters, is a real song.

You can also tithe with a credit card nowadays, and that seems almost too convenient and impersonal, and most churches—even the little white frame country churches where you can still hear an occasional "Amen!" from the back row—have adopted progressive attitudes toward air-conditioning.

So it's more comfortable in church today, but air-conditioning giveth, and air-conditioning taketh away. Gone for good are those paper fans with the wooden handles that were always available in the hymnal racks on the backs of pews.

It never bothered me to be hot in church because I thought being hot in church was a part of God's Great Plan. Sweat it out, brother, because that's just a sample of what awaits the backslider.

Down home on an August Sunday morning, the church is packed, and the message from the pulpit is fire and brimstone, and the congregation squirms as one.

You can *feel* the fire. You can *smell* the brimstone, and the closer the preacher gets to the everlasting flames, the faster the fat ladies in their print dresses fan themselves.

But there were other uses for church fans besides fanning away the Devil and the dog-day heat. You could swat noisy children and flies with church fans.

"Goat" Rainwater used to chew on the wooden handles, but "Goat" was always chewing on something like pencils or crayons. My mother said he probably had a vitamin deficiency.

A person could also learn a lot from a church fan. I learned what heaven looks like. The fans in our church were provided by the local funeral parlor, and at election time, a politician or two would bring in a batch.

On one side of a church fan would always be a picture of Jesus sitting with children and a lamb or two and a pony in a soft meadow near a brook.

That was obviously heaven to an eight-year-old, and I would stare at that picture during the sermon and wonder if pony rides were free when you crossed over Jordan. Certainly, I finally decided. That's why they call it "heaven."

On the other side would be the commercial message of the funeral parlor or the politician who had placed the fans.

"Hillside Funeral Home. All Insurance Policies Honored. Twenty-four Hour Ambulance Service. Ask About Our Chapel Rates."

Or, "Elect Buster Knowles State Senator. Veteran. Family man. Deacon. Honest."

Buster Knowles wasted a lot of money providing church fans, because he was never elected. He always included his smiling countenance on his fans, and he looked too much like the crooked Indian agent on "Tales of Wells Fargo."

Fortunately, I have what is probably one of the last church fans. A person who knows of my concern for their demise gave me one, and I am forever in his debt.

One Sunday soon, I may even take my fan to church, and in case the sermon runs a little long, I can stare peacefully at the picture of heaven while the rest of the congregation sweats through a hell of a thought:

God and Jimmy the Greek forbid, but if the preacher doesn't stop in five minutes, there goes the opening segment of "The NFL Today."

The Last of the
North Georgia
Trout Hounds

Another dog story, mostly true.

nSuches, Ga.
ever take a dog trout fishing. I know that; all experienced trout fishpersons like myself know that.

But the dog, who lived up on the hill from where I was hiding from civilization, had followed me around all day and we had become fast friends.

The dog had a number of pleasing characteristics, one of which was he didn't beg or whine when I opened a can of Vienna sausages and a package of soda crackers for lunch.

I despise begging, whining dogs. Plus, I despise sharing my Vienna sausages and soda crackers with any living thing.

Ah! The North Georgia mountains in the springtime. I am in a peaceful valley with a trout stream running through it. In the morning, a mist hangs over the valley, but soon the sun will burn the mist away and the brilliant surroundings will look as if they belong on an artist's canvas.

The afternoons are for rocking on a porch and for dozing off and for wondering why, if such settings are so gorgeous and peaceful, so many of us insist upon living in cities.

Maybe the answer had come from a young member of the family up the hill who owns the dog. She had mentioned that she will be graduating soon from the little high school down the mountain. I asked her what her plans would be afterwards.

"Leaving," she answered. "The only thing to do around here is raise collards."

I said raising collards was an honorable and worthwhile endeavor, but I don't think she heard me. We all go off to cities when we are young, because we don't know any better.

Then, we never quite summon the courage to get back out, because we can't get used to the idea of living more than four blocks from a convenience store.

Back to the dog. As sundown approached, it was time I tried to remove some of the trout from the stream. The dog followed me.

The reason you don't take a dog trout fishing is because dogs bark and scare off all the fish. I didn't read that anywhere. It is just a fact of nature that makes perfect sense to me.

"Go back," I shouted at the dog, but the dog ignored me.

I waded into the stream and made my first cast. The dog waded into the stream, too. One of two things was happening.

Either the dog had become so fond of me, he had to be at my side every moment, or I had stumbled upon one of the rarest of all breeds of dogs, the long-eared, North Georgia trout hound.

I'll keep this short. I waded on up the stream, and the dog waded with me, and, sure enough, the dog had a barking attack and so much for catching any fish.

I gave up after an hour and walked back to my porch and started rocking again, the dog still at my side. Soon, however, I heard the people up the hill call the dog to his dinner.

The dog forgot about our comradeship in the stream and his infatuation with me and left me alone with another can of Vienna sausages and another package of soda crackers, which the dog obviously didn't care for in the first place. Neither did I at the moment. I had planned on trout.

Later, as deep night fell over the valley, I wished for just a moment I was back home in the city. The city does have its advantages, you know. One is that I live only four blocks from a Del Taco.

I hope they fed that damned dog collards.

205

Gobbledygook

*A warm Thanksgiving message about how to get
even with a turkey of a neighbor.*

i have no idea what finally became of the old coot, but I
always think of him around Thanksgiving because he was the first
turkey I ever met.

I'm not certain of the exact characteristics of a person who
qualifies as a turkey, but I can spot a turkey person when I see or
hear one.

Jerry Brown, governor of California, is a turkey, for instance.
So are Anita Bryant and Reggie Jackson, the ballplayer, and
anybody who would go on television to advertise his used car lot.

The aforementioned old coot was really a turkey, however,
because besides being utterly obnoxious and full of any number of
unmentionable stuffings, he also raised turkeys.

Turkey turkeys, the kind that have feathers and make dumb,
gobbling sounds.

He was our neighbor when I was a kid, if you can call
somebody who constantly complains and constantly makes a
nuisance of himself a neighbor.

He lived in a large, white house. His back yard was where he
kept his turkeys, maybe 300 of them. His pen bordered my
grandfather's bean patch.

Let me tell you some things about turkeys:

- Turkeys don't have very much to do, so they gobble a lot.
- One turkey gobbling isn't a problem. Three hundred
turkeys gobbling at once, twenty-four hours a day, is enough to
wake the dead and drive the living slap crazy.

- Turkeys smell.
- Turkeys are easily spooked.
- A nervous turkey is a skinny turkey. That costs the turkey farmer money and makes him nervous.
- There is nothing more impossible to deal with than a nervous turkey farmer.

One of the local churches saved its money and bought a new bell. Our turkey farmer neighbor complained every time the church rang its new bell.

It spooked his precious turkeys.

My grandfather had a tractor. He used it in his bean patch, which bordered the turkey pen. Whenever my grandfather would plow in his bean patch, out would come the featherbrain, ranting and raving.

The sound of the tractor bothered his stupid turkeys.

I used to play a game in my front yard. I would throw rocks into the air and hit them with a broomstick and make believe I was a member of the 1959 Dodgers lining a shot off the wall at Comisky Park against the White Sox in the World Series.

One afternoon, Duke Snider ripped an Early Wynn hanging curveball over the bean patch and over the fence into the turkey pen.

The rock caught an unsuspecting turkey flush. Now, there was one less turkey to gobble all night, but I had to pay for the damage by handing over my allowance to gobblebrain for six months.

There was, however, one subsequent moment of revenge. In the stillness of the midnight, a child who shall remain nameless crept across my grandfather's bean patch to the turkey pen.

He lit an entire pack of Black Cat firecrackers and threw them in amongst the turkeys.

"Gobblegobblegobblegobblegobble!" went the turkeys.

"Arrrrrrrrrgh!" screamed the angry turkey farmer running out of his house still in his pajamas.

You, of course, will be eating turkey Thursday. I'll just have a ham sandwich and laugh at the satisfying memory of once having watched 299 turkeys and one old buzzard have a group nervous breakdown. Feathers may still be flying.

10
Womenfolk

One Rear End to Another

I received a very nice letter from Ann Landers after this article appeared. She thanked me for mentioning her name and then gave me some of her famous advice: "Find yourself another line of work."

i never miss Ann Landers in the newspaper because she always has an answer for any questions you can imagine:

"Dear Ann Landers,

"My husband came home last night with lipstick on his collar. When I asked him about it, he said he didn't know how it got there. I knew he was lying, so I broke his arm.

"Did I react too strongly, or should I have broken his other arm, too?—Big Hilda, Syracuse."

"Dear Big Hilda,

"It depends. If this was the first time your husband came home with lipstick on his collar, I would have to say you may have overreacted. A good punch in the belly would probably have sufficed.

"But if he makes a habit of coming home with such 'evidence' showing, I think you may have let the little worm off lightly."

The other day I was reading Ann Landers' column, and there was a letter from a woman in White Plains who asked:

"What is happening to our culture with so much emphasis on female rear ends? A person can't turn on the TV without seeing a close-up of a woman's derriere."

To which Ann Landers answered, astoundingly: "I don't have the slighest idea."

Imagine Ann Landers being stumped!

Frankly, it wasn't that tough a question. The woman from White Plains told Ann Landers she had seen an ad for jeans on television that had "popped my eyeballs."

She also said she had seen other ads for things like fanny smoothers, fanny shapers, and fanny padders.

"What," the woman went on, "is the explanation for this intense preoccupation with the fanny?"

I'll take it from here, Ann.

This "intense preoccupation" with the fanny is really nothing new. Men have always ogled women's most movable part, and with the new assertive attitude of the modern-day woman, we have learned the male hindpart is quite interesting to the female.

As far as more female rears on television these days, the answer there is simple:

Women buy a lot of things that have to do with their rears—jeans, pantyhose, girdles, diet foods, disco records—and men don't care what is being sold as long as they get a good look at a nice pair of hips occasionally.

There is one commercial that immediately comes to mind. Two women are discussing a particular undergarment that leaves no tell-tale rings or bulges when they walk around in their tight-fitting slacks.

But you never see the two women. All you see is their rear ends.

FIRST REAR END: You don't look like you are wearing anything underneath your tight-fitting slacks.

SECOND REAR END: Of course I am, silly. I'm wearing new Underwonders. No tell-tale rings, no bulges, and the freedom they give me is just fantastic!

A lot of people, like the woman in White Plains, might think a commercial with two talking rear ends is dumb and tasteless, but I'll take it any day over the one where you see the inside of a pipe being unclogged by a glob of Drano.

There is nothing dirty about the human tushy, and unless it reaches double-wide, mobile home proportions, it can be a thing of beauty.

I would advise the woman from White Plains to go water her petunias and stop sweating the small stuff. And I find it rather refreshing, incidentally, that the world's biggest know-it-all, Ann Landers, sometimes falls flat on her can just like the rest of us.

When
You Gotta
Go

It is my understanding that the female employees at Cagle Poultry Company and their management finally came to an agreement on who could go to the restroom when and for how long. Behold, another victory for human understanding.

i am having a difficult time deciding which side to take in the great debate at a Macon poultry processing plant over employees' restroom privileges.

Nearly two hundred workers have walked off their jobs at the Cagle Poultry Company after the plant manager, a man, sent around a memorandum advising the workers, mostly women-persons, that terrible things could happen to them if they didn't cool it on trips to the company restrooms.

Length of visits also get a mention. One company official was quoted as saying time wasted by employees in the restroom had cost his firm "thousands of dollars."

I don't doubt that. Over the years, I have noticed women tend to spend a great portion of their lives inside restrooms.

You take ball games and concerts. Rarely are there lines to the men's rooms at ball games and concerts. But there are always lines to the women's.

I have no idea what a woman does once inside a restroom at a ball game or concert, but it takes forever if you are waiting for one to come out.

214

Previously, I have been squarely behind the idea of installing a thirty-second clock inside women's restrooms.

On the other hand, there are some areas where I believe the less rules and regulations, the better for all concerned. Restrooms are one of those areas.

Through one of my reliable sources in Macon, I have obtained a copy of the Cagle Poultry Company memorandum involving "abuse of emergency restroom privileges." Those privileges, notes the memorandum, are spelled out precisely in Plant Rule No. 39.

The memorandum was signed by Malcolm Clark, plant manager, who issued the following new guidelines:

"Any employee will be allowed to visit the bathroom eight times in any four-week period, with a five-trip limit in any two-week period of the four weeks.

"Maximum time away from job is five minutes."

Mr. Clark also stated what would happen to those radicals who didn't follow his new guidelines:

"First offense: Verbal warning.

"Second offense: Written warning.

"Third offense: Three days off without pay.

"Fourth offense: Discharge."

That's not all. The crafty plant manager has also devised a way to insure that workers do not abuse their five-minute restroom time limit.

Each employee is to be issued a "bathroom card"—or "B-card"—to be kept in a rack next to a time clock outside the restrooms. It is to be the responsibility of all employees to clock in upon entering the restroom and to clock out once their business has been conducted.

"Special guards" are to make sure nobody tries anything tricky.

"First offense: Disciplinary layoff.

215

"Second offense: Discharge."

There is, of course, the sticky situation of employees who have to visit the restrooms in order to take medicine. Mr. Clark thought of that.

The memorandum states that if an employee needs additional visits to take medicine, the employee must have a note from a doctor. If after three weeks the problem is not corrected, the employee gets a leave of absence to correct it.

Company officials weren't talking to reporters Friday. Workers said the rules were "unjust and demeaning." Both sides were meeting—along with Labor Department representatives—to work out a possible solution.

Don't compromise, girls. I think I have decided whom to back here. Work me like a dog. Cut my pay. Steal my pension. But tell me I can't go to the restroom when I'm damn good and ready, and you can take Plant Rule No. 39 and flush it.

Will You Still Respect Me in the Morning?

Quite frankly, I never saw anything wrong with a woman calling me for a date. In fact, I encouraged it. I wonder why nobody ever called?

One of the papers last week ran a series of articles for its women readers entitled "How to Meet Men . . . Now That You Are Liberated."

One part of the series caught my eye because it was about how a liberated, single woman should go about asking a man for a date and what she should suggest they do if he accepts.

"Why should a woman sit passively by the telephone waiting for a man to call her for a date?" the author—apparently a liberated, single woman—asked.

"No reason," she answered herself, "when the woman can make the first move."

I agree. And as a single male, I would more than welcome women calling me to ask for dates. I have spent a great portion of my life calling to ask them.

I want revenge.

I want *them* to hear what mocking, hysterical laughter sounds like on the other end of the telephone.

I want *them* to feel the pangs of regret and embarrassment when a voice says, "You must be outta your mind, Horseface."

I want *them* to experience the intense rejection when the

object of their affection suggests further efforts would be fruitless, as in "Bug me one more time, creep, and I'm calling the cops."

It's no picnic asking people for dates, you know, and I simply do not understand why so many of the women I have honored with an offer of my company have thought it necessary to respond abruptly and often downright crudely.

But forget the revenge. I hold no grudges. I will even make it as easy for you as I possibly can.

Don't sit around pondering over what to suggest for our rendezvous if I see fit to accept your invitation. Over the years, I have suggested a number of fun and clever things I like to do on dates.

As you will see, the dimwitted women who have turned down these opportunities don't know a good time when they are handed one on a silver platter.

When calling, order by number, please:

1. COOKING MY SUPPER: My favorite meal is country fried steak smothered in sawmill gravy, creamed potatoes, butterbeans, squash, spring onions, thinly sliced tomatoes, and unsweetened ice tea.

After supper, do not worry about thinking of something else for us to do. After a meal like that, I would prefer to lie down on the couch and take a little siesta.

2. RUB MY BACK.

3. WATCHING BALL GAMES ON TV: One of my favorite things to do on a date. Make sure the beer is cold and plenty of snacks are within reaching distance of my seat in front of the television.

If you would prefer to do something else while I watch the ball game, that is fine. Just be sure you're back in time to start the fire in the grill.

4. DOING MY LAUNDRY: When you have a break between cycles, maybe I could tell you some of my favorite jokes.

218

5. HANGING OUT WITH SOME OF MY FRIENDS: We'd treat you just like one of the guys, unless we decided to go to a beer joint, of course. You could wait in the car and read one of those women's magazines that tell you how to avoid getting stretch marks.

6. FISHING: I like to fish, but I do not like to bait my hook, because sometimes when you stick a hook into a Louisiana Pink, they squirt at you. If you will bait my hook for me, I'll let you borrow my new scaler when you clean the fish.

7. WASHING MY TRUCK: Real fun on an afternoon date. Afterwards, we'll go for a spin. I would let you ride up front with me, but that's where my dog sits.

8. LISTENING TO MY ALBUMS: Soft lights and the Statler Brothers. This is what I do when I feel really romantic. Another glass of Ripple, my pet?

9. GOING BOWLING: Lots of laughs and it won't cost you much, except for the beer I drink and shoe rentals.

10. FOOLING AROUND: But promise you'll still respect me in the morning.

Mayor
Hot
Lips

This was one of my favorite political stories of the year. Incidentally, it had a happy ending. Teddy Kennedy rode Jane Byrne's endorsement to a bellyflop in the Illinois Democratic primary.

Chicago Mayor Jane Byrne's leap from the Carter camp to the Ted Kennedy fold obviously has major political implications for the 1980 presidential election. But it also says something else scary.

It says that men, even the president of the United States, are still stupid when it comes to reading the intentions of women.

To get the full impact of the situation, let us review exactly what happened in the Byrne-to-Carter-and-then-to-Kennedy escapade:

A few weeks ago, President Carter got all dressed up in his tuxedo and flew to Chicago to appear at a fund-raising dinner for Mayor Byrne.

Mayor Byrne got all dressed up, too. She wore her white party dress. And a good time was had by all.

Mayor Byrne said she thought the president was a swell guy and knocked everybody on his tomato aspic by saying—so the Carter people thought—she would support her dinner guest for the 1980 Democratic nomination.

President Carter then strode to the podium and talked about what a terrific job Mayor Byrne is doing in Chicago and promised her some big federal grants for her city.

The back-scratching out of the way, Mayor Byrne then kissed the president. I saw her do it on television. She put one smack on the old boy, and he grinned from the Loop to downtown Gary, Indiana.

"Do you think she really meant it when she said she would support you?" an aide asked the president on the flight back to Washington.

"How can you ask such a question?" the president shot back. "She kissed me, didn't she?"

It was only a matter of days before Mayor Byrne had announced she had changed her mind and would now lend her support and that of the Chicago Democratic "machine" to Ted Kennedy.

President Carter should have known better, of course, but then he is just a man, and men are always naive when it comes to being kissed by women.

Men have always thought if a woman kisses you, it means something special. It means she is your girl, she will go with you to the prom, she will give you something nice for your birthday, she will hold your hand in the moonlight.

She won't go around kissing everybody else.

Baloney. I still remember my first kiss. It was from Kathy Sue Loudermilk, the school sex symbol. I felt the earth move.

What I really felt was a half-dozen other guys lining up to be next.

What women have always known about men is that if you kiss one of the big oafs, he'll be eating out of the palm of your hand.

I had hoped that when a woman reached the high position of mayor of a major city, she would no longer resort to such tactics, but Mayor Byrne's plot is evidence I was only dreaming.

The president came courting, and Mayor Byrne played him for the fool. She cooed and smiled and lured him into her web and then "sealed" their new partnership with a kiss.

221

My Chicago sources tell me Mayor Byrne has used this technique all along. Since she has been mayor, they say, she has kissed practically everybody in town, including a number of city officials who thought getting kissed by the mayor was a sign of job security, only to find their desks cleaned out and the doors to their offices locked while the mayor's lip prints were still fresh on their cheeks.

Whether Ted Kennedy can keep Her Two-Facedness on his side remains to be seen, but at least the Kennedy people are trying to learn from the Carter mistake and the mistake men have been making since the Garden of Eden.

A memorandum has been circulated from Kennedy campaign headquarters to all male Kennedy workers and to the senator himself, detailing rules to follow in case of any contact with Mayor Byrne of Chicago.

"If she puckers," goes Rule No. 1, "run for your life."

Plowing Up the Cornrows

I wonder if women really appreciate it when men take the time to give them guidance and counseling like this:

normally, I try to refrain from any comment concerning the latest in women's fashions and style. There are a couple of reasons for that.

One, my taste in that area tends to be a bit tacky. For example, I miss the hot-pants-and-white-boots look, and there is nothing like a dame in short shorts and high heels.

Two, it doesn't do any good to tell women what they should wear and how they should look. Women simply won't listen to such constructive criticism.

If women would listen, we would never have had to endure the sack dress and that awful period when all coeds were wearing baggy blue jeans, sweatshirts, and combat boots in an apparent effort to look like female versions of "Skag" on the way to the blast furnace.

Despite all this, however, I no longer can remain a silent observer, because now women are doing something really stupid. I don't care how many letters and calls I get from fire-breathing feminists, I'm going to say this anyway:

The Bo Derek braided look, the "cornrow" hairstyle that apparently is about to sweep the nation, is absolutely hideous.

Allow me to bring those who have been sleeping for a couple

of months, or who don't read *People* magazine or watch the Phil Donahue TV show, up to date.

This movie called *10* came out, see. It starred a young woman named Bo Derek, who since has become the nation's latest lust-object, replacing Farrah and the blonde cutie on "WKRP" and other assorted, curvaceous airheads.

The movie's plot would bore you, so all that is really necessary to know is that this "Bo" (silly name for a girl) wore her hair in "tightly woven plaits, laced with beads," as *People* magazine described it.

I can describe it better. As appealing as the child most certainly is from the forehead down, her hair looked like somebody had made a terrible mistake.

Frankly, her hair looked like something the Chinese might use to count on, or the result of shampooing with Drano.

But this ridiculous Medusa-like hairstyle called the "cornrow"—a fairly appropriate name, I might add—is spreading like a bad case of dandruff, and it must be stopped. Otherwise, we might soon be up to our eyeballs in once-attractive women who have all become rope-heads.

There are plenty of reasons, my sisters, not to give in to what is nothing more than a Hollywood-bred fad. Please pay attention while I list them:

1. If you want to make yourself appear to have just hit town from another planet, there is a method much less drastic than having your hair cornrowed. Have one of your eyes moved to the middle of your head, for instance.

2. A cornrow at most Hollywood beauty salons can cost as much as $400, says *People,* and can take up to ten hours to complete. For four hundred smackers, you can have your entire chassis rebuilt with money left over for four new pairs of pantyhose.

224

3. Cicely Tyson, the brilliant actress, also is a gorgeous woman. There was a picture of Cicely Tyson in *People* magazine with her hair in cornrows. She looked a lot like Stevie Wonder.

4. Cordie Mae Poovy, a girl in my school, was the first female in this country to wear her hair in cornrows. That's because her father ran a dairy farm and one afternoon she got her head caught in one of the milking machines. We used to spend recess throwing rocks at Cordie Mae Poovy.

5. Experts are saying if you wear your hair in a cornrow for too long, all you hair might fall out.

6. I hope it does.

My
Angel

I gave Billy Bob Bailey the honor of announcing my third marriage, which occurred on February 10, 1980. At this writing, some six months later, we are still blissfully happy. And they said it wouldn't last . . .

bFort Deposit, Ala.

illy Bob Bailey is my name and plumbing is my game. People around here like to say, "If it'll stop up, ol' Billy Bob can unclog it."

They got that right. You take Mrs. Arlene Watts' kitchen sink. Mrs. Watts, a lovely child who was once named Miss Fort Deposit Seed and Feed Show Princess, has had all sorts of problems with her kitchen sink lately.

As a matter of fact, that sucker has backed up every afternoon for two weeks, and Billy Bob has been out to her house every day for hours at the time, and I've just about wore my new auger slap out.

I think I finally got the job completed, though, and I'd bet my dog Rooster against a one-eyed mule that sink don't back up again for at least six months, which is just about the time Arlene's—I mean, Mrs. Watts'—husband, Harvey, will have to go out of town again.

But my problem ain't what you're interested in readin' about today, so sit back and get ready for some of Billy Bob's best writin'.

226

As many of you know, plumbing ain't my only talent. I also write a column for the local weekly called, "The Straight Flush with Billy Bob," and people down here think I hung the journalism moon.

I get to write occasionally in your big Atlanta paper, too, because that scoundrel Lewis Grizzard is always needin' me to bail him out, like the time he said he had come down with some mysterious illness.

He comes down with a lot of mysterious illnesses, just about every time he goes out and tries to drink all the see-through whiskey north of Bainbridge. If it flows downhill, that fool will put ice in it and try to drink it.

But this is a special occasion, indeed. Y'all have heard the rumors.

The boy did it, folks. Got married. It happened right here in Fort Deposit, Aladamnbama, last Sunday afternoon.

Grizzard couldn't get a license in Georgia because up there you have to list all your previous marriages. Georgia doesn't give you enough lines for Grizzard to put all his down.

In Alabama, you just have to list your latest foul-up and the reason for it. By "reason," Grizzard put down, "She kept burnin' the cornbread."

It was a nice ceremony. The bride wore red. I was the best man, of course, and Rooster helped get everybody seated and then bit the bride's daddy when he made a complete fool of himself as soon as the preacher got to that part about, "If anybody here has any objections to this marriage . . . . "

After the wedding, there was a reception over at the diner, and everybody in Fort Deposit must have come, because it took six pairs of jumper cables to get that crowd cranked and out of there when it was over.

Rooster said he thought the best thing they served was the individually wrapped Slim-Jims and the fried chicken necks, but

227

don't pay much attention to him because that dog will eat anything he can outrun.

There was also a beautiful ice-carving of a possum, and the cold duck they brought over from the Moose Club was dee-vine.

Of course, everybody wants to know why Grizzard decided to do it again. That boy gets married like most folks eat popcorn.

Well, I can tell you why he did it. I knew the answer when I saw him watchin' his new bride pour quarters in the jukebox with one hand and hold a longneck Blue in the other.

"Listen to what she plays," he said, all moon-eyed.

The girl may not have any taste in men, but she knows her music. She played a little Conway, followed that with Willie, and then she played that new song that goes, "We used to kiss on the mouth, but it's all over now."

"Can she cook, too?" I asked the groom.

"Can George Corley Wallace sing 'Dixie'?" Grizzard asked me back.

That's all I needed to know. Number Three likes country music and her beer in a bottle, she won't burn the cornbread, and I didn't get a close look, but it appeared to me she's still got all her teeth, too.

I thought ol' Lewis put it as good as it could be put when he looked up at me, still sober at the time, and said, "I didn't have no choice. An angel don't come by every day."

You Can Call Me "Papa," or You Can Call Me . . .

Father's Day doesn't have anything to do with "Womenfolk," which is the name of this chapter. On second thought, if it weren't for womenfolk, Father's Day would be just another Sunday.

Sunday was my first Father's Day. What I mean is, Sunday was my first time to be a father on Father's Day.

That's not exactly right, either. What I am is a stepfather, but my stepchildren are young—seven and four—so they didn't know any better than to give me a gift anyway.

I was hoping for a case of imported beer. I got socks. I always get socks when I wish for beer.

Let me tell you about my stepchildren.

The seven-year-old is a girl. The four-year-old isn't. Their average age is 5.5, which means there is a great deal of yelling and screaming and whining and crying at my house. My wife, their mother, is constantly yelling and screaming and whining and crying.

I think that comes with being the mother of two children at the age where they are trying to give everybody around them a nervous breakdown.

I came home from work and found my wife in tears. I asked her what was wrong. She said the four-year-old had run away.

"Don't cry," I said. "He'll come back."

"He already did," she replied. "Why do you think I'm crying?"

Actually, my stepchildren don't bother me that much. Whenever they get out of control, I go down to the bus station and buy a ticket for someplace like Butte, Montana. I never get on the bus, but it is comforting to know I could in case something drastic happened, like the four-year-old finding out where I hid his Big Wheel.

Those of you who do not live around children may not know what a Big Wheel is. It is a tricycle-like vehicle made of plastic. When it is pedaled across pavement by a four-year-old, it makes a sound unbearable to the adult ear.

Gestapo agents used small children riding Big Wheels to force information from captives during World War II.

I've been a stepfather for four months. The first big decision a family has to make when a stepfather moves in is what the children should call him.

We discussed "Papa," but "Papa" sounds about sixty and German. I am neither.

"Big Daddy" was one of my suggestions, but my wife pointed out I have nothing in common with Burl Ives in *Cat on a Hot Tin Roof*, including his money, so we threw out that one.

Finally, we decided the children should call me by my real name, "Lewis." My wife, who doesn't have to be that respectful, gets to call me by my nickname, which is "Hey, You."

The first order of business a stepfather must handle when he takes responsibility for stepchildren is to bring a new sense of discipline into their lives.

I am a stern disciplinarian. Last week, the seven-year-old wanted to run away and get married. I said, sternly, "You'll have to ask your mother first."

I must admit children have been an adjustment for me after my years of bachelorhood, and I would not be totally truthful if I said there weren't times I ask myself how the devil I wound up a daddy when my fastball is basically intact.

But being a stepfather isn't something a man should take lightly. If you will pardon my sentimentality for a moment, I know a man who became one twenty-five years ago, and he still offers advice and guidance to a stepson about to ride off the backside of his thirties.

For the sake of the two stepchildren who live under my roof, my Father's Day prayer for 1980 is that I can do half for them what my stepfather did for me.